THE COMING
SIGNS OF OUR TIMES

The Coming
SIGNS OF OUR TIMES

A Guide for Those Who Are Left Behind in the Generation of Tribulation

MICHAEL SAWDY

**BIBLICAL SIGNS
PUBLISHING**

Published in Plymouth, Michigan, by Biblical Signs Publishing, an imprint of BiblicalSigns.com.

This Book may be purchased in bulk for educational, business, fund-raising, or sales promotional use. For information, please email BiblicalSigns@gmail.com.

Unless otherwise noted, Scripture quotations in this book are taken from the King James or English Standard Versions. Public domain.

All italics in Scripture quotations were added by the author for emphasis.

ISBN 9780578595535

Library of Congress Control Number: 2019917193

Cover Design by MichaEL Sawdy.

Printed in the United States of America

TO THE "LEFT BEHIND":

You are in possession of this book because a loved one, who has been raptured to be with the Lord, cared deeply about the salvation of your eternal soul. More importantly, you are reading this book because the God whom you didn't care too much for throughout your life is giving you a second chance to get to Heaven. It is my prayer that the words of this book will lead you to our Lord Jesus Christ, and that you will then spend the next seven years leading others to Him as well. The time has come to make the most important decision of your entire life, and I hope this book helps you to make the right choice. Choose faith. Choose Jesus!

CONTENTS

INTRODUCTION: LEFT BEHIND?   9

CHAPTER I: 4 HORSEMEN OF THE APOCALYPSE   17

CHAPTER II: FIFTH AND SIXTH SEALS   25

CHAPTER III: 144,000 JEWISH EVANGELISTS SEALED   33

CHAPTER IV: SEVENTH SEAL AND FOUR TRUMPETS   39

CHAPTER V: FIFTH AND SIXTH TRUMPETS   47

CHAPTER VI: THE ANTICHRIST   57

CHAPTER VII: THE FALSE PROPHET   73

CHAPTER VIII: MARK OF THE BEAST   79

CHAPTER IX: THIRD TEMPLE AND TWO WITNESSES   87

CHAPTER X: 7TH TRUMPET - 7 VIALS - 7 PLAGUES   95

CHAPTER XI: BABYLON THE GREAT IS FALLEN   107

CHAPTER XII: ARMAGEDDON AND CHRIST'S RETURN   127

EPILOGUE: A NEW HEAVEN AND A NEW EARTH   135

ACKNOWLEDGMENTS   143

NOTES   145

ABOUT THE AUTHOR   149

INTRODUCTION

LEFT BEHIND?

I WILL SHEW THEE THINGS WHICH MUST BE HEREAFTER.

- REVELATION 4:1

IF YOU'RE READING THIS, it is for one of two reasons. Either you have opened this book *before* the Rapture of Christ's Church, because you desire to have a greater understanding of Revelation and the Tribulation that is described therein, *or* there has been a mysterious mass disappearance of your Christian loved ones and you're searching for answers. Let me begin by addressing the first group of readers - those reading this book prior to the Rapture.

I am sure there are a few questions that some of you want to ask, like how can I be so convinced of a Pre-Tribulation Rapture? And why am I so sure that we will not go through the seven-year Tribulation with the rest of humanity? To answer these questions, I would suggest that you read the Introduction of my previous book - *Even More Signs of Our Times: MORE Biblical Reasons Why This Could Be the Generation of the Rapture.* I think that my arguments for a Pre-Trib evacuation were Biblically-sound and concrete. There is also one big scriptural reason in particular I'd recently discovered that solidifies my belief that the Church won't be going through the Tribulation period. The Spirit revealed the powerful Pre-Trib proof to me during my research for this book.

If you're a Christian who's held to the Mid-Trib or Post-Trib points of view about the Rapture, I believe this strong and simple argument may well change your mind. While the Tribulation is described throughout the pages of the Holy Bible (both Old and New Testaments), the most detailed description of the seven-year period of Hell on Earth is found in the Book of Revelation. It was through my thorough study of the Book that the Spirit highlighted for me the fact that "the Church" (global body of Bible-believing Christians) is *not present* during any judgments of the Tribulation.

There are 22 Chapters comprising the Revelation to John. In those Chapters, you'll discover that *the Church* is only mentioned at the beginning of the Book (*before* Tribulation judgments begin to fall), and not mentioned again until the end of the Book (*after* the judgments have passed). Upon reading the first few Chapters for yourself, you will find the last time the Church is mentioned is in Revelation 3:22. It is in the *very next verse* where the Rapture event is possibly described. Compare Revelation 4:1 with some of the most quoted Rapture verses in the Bible, which are found in the Book of 1st Thessalonians -

"AFTER THIS I LOOKED, AND, BEHOLD, A DOOR WAS OPENED IN HEAVEN: AND THE FIRST **VOICE** WHICH I HEARD WAS AS IT WERE OF A **TRUMPET** TALKING WITH ME; WHICH SAID, **COME UP HITHER** (COME UP HERE), AND I WILL SHEW THEE THINGS WHICH MUST BE HEREAFTER." - REVELATION 4:1

"FOR THE LORD HIMSELF SHALL DESCEND FROM HEAVEN WITH A SHOUT, WITH THE **VOICE** OF THE ARCHANGEL, AND WITH THE **TRUMP** OF GOD: AND THE DEAD IN CHRIST SHALL RISE FIRST: THEN WE WHICH ARE ALIVE AND REMAIN SHALL BE **CAUGHT UP** TOGETHER WITH THEM IN THE CLOUDS, TO MEET THE LORD **IN THE AIR**: AND SO SHALL WE EVER BE WITH THE LORD. WHEREFORE COMFORT ONE ANOTHER WITH THESE WORDS." - 1ST THESSALONIANS 14:16-18

Notice the similarities? Both pieces of Scripture speak of the voice, trumpet, and going up to Heaven. If you are still a Pre-Trib skeptic, then explain why the Church is not mentioned again until the FINAL Chapter of Revelation (22:16).

Many who believe in a Mid-Trib or Post-Trib Rapture like to point to Bible-believers being martyred during the 7-year period, and these martyrs are referred to as the "Tribulation saints." I'll write in greater detail about this group later in the book, but you need to read the Book of Revelation in context. There are 144,000 Messianic Jewish Evangelists, of the Twelve Tribes of Israel, who will be sealed and filled with the Holy Spirit to preach the Gospel during the Tribulation. They will bring an innumerable multitude of souls to Christ in a very short period of time. The fruit of their ministry is recorded in Revelation 7:9-17. The *Tribulation saints* are those who come to faith in Christ DURING the Tribulation, through the preaching of the 144,000.

This group of saints is never once referred to as "the Church," as believers most always were throughout the pages of the New Testament since the day of Pentecost. I ask anyone who doubts a Pre-Trib Rapture to explain how the Church is *absent* from the majority of one of the longest books in the New Testament, which just so happens to be *every single* Chapter where the greatest Tribulation on Planet Earth is described! I pray that this powerful argument for true believers being kept out of the Tribulation Hour (Revelation 3:10) quells any fears that you may have been feeling about coming events of the End Times. If you're a believer in the Lord Jesus Christ, then there is never anything to fear!

On the other hand, for those reading this who have been left behind, there *is* reason to fear. But the main reason I have written this book is to let you know that there is STILL HOPE. You can *still be saved,* and you can be reunited with your loved ones in Heaven someday. I'm sure some of you are probably saying, wait a minute, aren't those of us who have been left behind destined to endure the judgments of God that you Christians always warned about? Aren't we left behind to be punished for rejecting Jesus? The answers to these questions would be both yes *and* no. I say yes, because you willingly rejected Christ when you had heard it preached that He was the Savior of your soul. You had ignored or flat-out refused to believe JOHN 3:16 -

"FOR GOD SO LOVED THE WORLD, THAT HE GAVE HIS ONLY BEGOTTEN SON, THAT WHOSOEVER BELIEVES IN HIM SHOULD NOT PERISH, BUT HAVE EVERLASTING LIFE."

I also said no, because God still loves you the exact same as when you'd heard the verse preached before. He's not willing that any should perish, but that *all* men everywhere should come to repentance (2nd Peter 3:9). While the worst tribulation the world has ever experienced is just on the horizon, take comfort that the LORD will preserve you through it. That is, of course, if you will humble yourself, repent of your sins, believe on the name of His Son Jesus, and surrender your life to Him. Once you become His child, you're guaranteed eternal life just as much as your raptured family and friends were. You can be just as saved as they were.

Your Christian loved ones had been counted worthy to escape the coming Tribulation because of the strong faith that they held firm to, even when people like you had mocked them. Don't beat yourself up over it too much though; because take a look around, there are a lot of people who lived just like you on Earth - aren't there? I'm guessing millions... maybe billions? The question you have to ask yourself is: are you still gonna live like an unbeliever, and continue on a highway to Hell - which draws closer each and every day? Seven years from now, that is where you will end up.

Wouldn't you rather live to see your loved ones again, spend eternity with them in Heaven, and tell them that their prayers for you were not in vain? If so, then this book will be your guide to ensure you can do that.

Search around and see if you can find the Holy Bible, because you're going to need one. If you can't find one in your home, then check homes of your vanished Christian family. If you still can't find it, then you'd better run out and buy one; because very soon it will be *banned*. It will also likely be a criminal offense to even possess the Holiest Book on Earth in the near future, so keep it someplace safe. You are entering into the time of the Antichrist. Very soon, all faiths will come together in a One-World-Religion. A majority of the citizens of Earth will worship the coming world leader *as God*, and you'll read much more about him in this book.

While you, and many like you, called us Christians "bigoted" and "closed-minded" for believing God's Word, you will be more than mocked and ridiculed. In the near future, you could actually be locked up or even put to death for preaching the words of the Bible. While that sounds scary, you *must* turn to Jesus. He is the only hope you have in making it out of the Tribulation alive; and I mean "alive" not just in a here and now sense, but *eternally*. You may be martyred for His Name, but you'll *live forever* thereafter. If you worship Antichrist, you'll not only die in this life, but your earthly death will be followed by an eternity of burning in the fire of Hell. My job is to make sure that you don't choose Door #2.

I am going to lay out all of the Biblical prophecies pertaining to the Tribulation, in order that you may know what's coming and can prepare accordingly. The event that will signal the start of the Tribulation period will be the brokering of a seven-year covenant of peace between Israel and her hostile Islamic neighbors. Bear in mind, the leader who forges the treaty will be the Antichrist.

"HE SHALL CONFIRM THE COVENANT WITH MANY FOR ONE WEEK (7 YEARS): AND IN THE MIDST OF THE WEEK (3 ½ YEARS) HE SHALL CAUSE THE SACRIFICE AND THE OBLATION TO CEASE, AND FOR THE OVERSPREADING OF ABOMINATIONS HE

WILL MAKE IT DESOLATE, EVEN UNTIL THE CONSUMMATION, AND THAT DETERMINED SHALL BE POURED UPON THE DESOLATE." - DANIEL 9:27

The covenant begins the countdown of the final seven years of this world as we have known it. The seven-year Tribulation is known as the *70th Week* of the Old Testament's Book of Daniel. In Chapter 9 of the prophetic book, the Angel Gabriel revealed to Daniel that 70 weeks remained in Israel's future; and each week prophetically contained seven years - similar to how a "week," as we know it, contains seven days. 69 weeks have been fulfilled, as we learn in Daniel 9:25-26 that the appearance of "Messiah the Prince" (Jesus) would take place at the close of the 69th week. It was also prophesied that Messiah would be put to death, and that the Holy City, Jerusalem, and Jewish Temple would be destroyed immediately after the 69th week.

"KNOW THEREFORE AND UNDERSTAND, THAT FROM THE GOING FORTH OF THE COMMANDMENT TO RESTORE AND TO BUILD JERUSALEM UNTO THE MESSIAH THE PRINCE SHALL BE SEVEN WEEKS, AND THREESCORE AND TWO WEEKS: THE STREET SHALL BE BUILT AGAIN, AND THE WALL, EVEN IN TROUBLOUS TIMES. AFTER THREESCORE AND TWO WEEKS (62) SHALL MESSIAH BE CUT OFF (PUT TO DEATH), BUT NOT FOR HIMSELF (SACRIFICED FOR SINS OF ALL MANKIND): AND THE PEOPLE OF THE PRINCE THAT SHALL COME (ROMAN EMPIRE) SHALL DESTROY THE CITY AND THE SANCTUARY (JERUSALEM AND THE HOLY TEMPLE)." - DANIEL 9:25-26

We know from history that Jesus was crucified in 33 AD, and that the Romans destroyed the Holy City and Temple in 70 AD. For nearly 1900 years following the destruction of Israel's Capital City, the Jews had been scattered all over the world; and the final seven years of Daniel's prophecy, found in Daniel 9:27, could not be fulfilled. In 1948, God fulfilled scores of prophetic promises to return the Jews to their ancient Biblical Homeland.

"THEREFORE SAY, THUS SAITH THE LORD GOD; I WILL EVEN GATHER YOU FROM THE PEOPLE, AND ASSEMBLE YOU OUT OF THE COUNTRIES WHERE YE HAVE BEEN SCATTERED, AND I WILL GIVE YOU THE LAND OF ISRAEL." - EZEKIEL 11:17

In 1967, the Israelis reunified their ancient City of Jerusalem. Antichrist is prophesied to sit in a rebuilt Jewish Holy Temple in Jerusalem, and will declare himself to be God in that place.

"HE OPPOSETH AND EXALTETH HIMSELF ABOVE ALL THAT IS CALLED GOD, OR THAT IS WORSHIPPED; SO THAT HE AS GOD SITTETH IN THE TEMPLE OF GOD, SHEWING HIMSELF THAT HE IS GOD." - 2ND THESSALONIANS 2:4

Without a Jewish Jerusalem and a Holy Temple under Israeli control, this prophecy could never be fulfilled. With Israel finally back in their Land, and again controlling their Holy City, the only thing that is missing is a Third Temple. I believe that Antichrist's seven-year covenant could allow for the Israelis to rebuild it. I'll go into more detail about this subject later in the book.

There are many people today who ask why there is such a long lull of time between the 69th and 70th weeks? The answer is *the Church.* For nearly 2,000 years, Jews and Gentiles all over the world have had the opportunity to come to Christ Jesus and *be saved.* Had the 70th week happened way back when, then none of us would be here. When Israel's history ends, world history as we know it will end! The Church Age is a gap between Daniel's 69th and 70th weeks. Once the very last sinner on Earth accepts Jesus as Lord, and is brought into His flock, the Church Age will end.

To those left behind: that is why the Rapture happened. The very last sinner to be saved was saved. Now, the LORD will again turn His attention to Israel - to bring the remnant of His chosen people to their Messiah, Yeshua HaMashiach (Jesus Christ).

"I WOULD NOT, BRETHREN, THAT YE SHOULD BE IGNORANT OF THIS MYSTERY, LEST YE SHOULD BE WISE IN YOUR OWN CONCEITS; THAT BLINDNESS IN PART HAPPENED TO ISRAEL, UNTIL THE FULNESS OF GENTILES COME IN." - ROMANS 11:25

The fulness of the Gentiles has come in, and the 70th week of Daniel (seven-year Tribulation) is about to begin. Are you ready? Most likely not. After reading this book, *you will be*. So, if you missed the Rapture, hope is not yet lost; but be prepared, because EVERYTHING IS ABOUT TO CHANGE.

FOR THEN SHALL BE GREAT TRIBULATION, SUCH AS WAS NOT SINCE THE BEGINNING OF THE WORLD TO THIS TIME, NO, NOR EVER SHALL BE. AND EXCEPT THOSE DAYS SHOULD BE SHORTENED, THERE SHOULD NO FLESH BE SAVED: BUT FOR THE ELECT'S SAKE THOSE DAYS SHALL BE SHORTENED.

- MATTHEW 24:21-22

CHAPTER ONE

4 HORSEMEN OF THE APOCALYPSE

I SAW WHEN THE LAMB OPENED ONE OF THE SEALS, AND I
HEARD, AS IT WERE THE NOISE OF THUNDER, ONE OF THE
FOUR BEASTS SAYING, COME AND SEE.

- REVELATION 6:1

THE OPENING OF THE seven-sealed book officially begins the Tribulation judgments on Planet Earth. Lord Jesus is the only one in Heaven who is found worthy to break the seals of the book that contains the long overdue judgments of God. During the Church Age, Christ was the one who saved us from God's wrath. During the Tribulation, He will become the *executor* of it. There will be three sets of judgments to be released upon the earth in multiples of seven, equating to the number of our God and Father, YHWH - 777. These will all take place throughout a seven-year period. As I've written in my past books, there is no denying that God loves the number 7; and it is never made more clear than in Revelation.

The *Seven* Seals will be followed by the *Seven* Trumpets, and then the *Seven* Vials (Bowls) of *seven* plagues will be poured out upon Earth in the culmination of the *seven* years of God's great wrath. The first four seals that Lord Jesus will break open release the infamous Four Horsemen of the Apocalypse, and the opening of the first seal brings forth the rider on the **WHITE HORSE** -

"AND I SAW, AND BEHOLD A WHITE HORSE: AND HE THAT SAT ON HIM HAD A BOW; AND A CROWN WAS GIVEN UNTO HIM: AND HE WENT FORTH CONQUERING, AND TO CONQUER." - REVELATION 6:2

This first horseman will be *Antichrist*. He will be an impostor of Jesus Christ - who just so happens to make His return to the earth on a *white horse* (Revelation 19:11). The color is symbolic of light, purity, and holiness - which are all attributes of our Lord. While I say that the rider is "Antichrist," he will definitely not be recognized as such upon his arrival on the world scene. He is said to come carrying a bow. The bow (opposed to sword) symbolizes that he'll initially come into the world as a peacemaker - imitating Christ, who is the Prince of Peace. The bow is symbolic of peace because the rainbow is what the LORD used to symbolize His Covenant with mankind.

This makes perfect sense, since the event that bridges the gap between the Rapture and the start of the Tribulation is the forging of a seven-year *covenant* of peace between Israel and her hostile Muslim neighbors (specifically Palestine) - which is brokered by the Antichrist. While most Bible believers know the truth about this great deceiver, the majority of those left behind will view him as a man of peace. They will praise and uplift him as a savior, and as the messiah of a world that's been thrown into chaos following the mysterious disappearance of much of the earth's population in the Rapture. No one that is ignorant to Biblical teaching will ever suspect him of being the most wicked leader to ever rise to power in the history of mankind.

"HE SHALL COME IN PEACEABLY, AND OBTAIN THE KINGDOM BY FLATTERIES." - DANIEL 11:21

He will do absolutely no wrong in their eyes. In fact, halfway through the seven-year Tribulation (when he begins to show his true colors and actually blasphemes the God of gods), instead of losing popularity among the citizens of the world, he will actually be worshipped by them *as God*. The crown that is given to him, in verse 2 of Revelation 6, implies that he'll be victorious over anyone who opposes him; and further proof of this can be found in the next phrase: "he went forth conquering, and to conquer." So, though he rises to power as a man of peace, he will eventually become hell-bent (no pun intended) on global conquest and world domination. There's much more to say about this rider, and you'll read about him all throughout this book - especially in chapter 6.

Now, I want to address the rider on the **RED HORSE** -

"WHEN HE OPENED THE SECOND SEAL, I HEARD THE SECOND BEAST SAY, COME AND SEE. AND THERE WENT OUT ANOTHER HORSE THAT WAS RED: AND POWER WAS GIVEN TO HIM THAT SAT THEREON TO TAKE PEACE FROM THE EARTH, AND THAT THEY SHOULD KILL ONE ANOTHER: AND THERE WAS GIVEN UNTO HIM A GREAT SWORD." - REVELATION 6:3-4

The opening of the second seal brings this second horseman, riding the red horse. The color symbolizes blood, and this rider will no doubt be responsible for the shedding of a lot of it. While the world enjoys a long-sought utopia brought about by the first rider, the second horseman will dash their hopes for world peace. Since Israel's covenant with their neighbors is not broken until 3 ½ years into the Tribulation, I don't think this rider will target the Jewish State. He is instead sent forth to bring violence, terrorism, and war to the rest of the earth. I suspect the result of this war and chaos - along with the famine, economic woes, plagues, and death that will be brought about by the next two riders - will be the first rider (Antichrist) seizing the global control that he desires.

He'll be viewed as the only leader who can bring peace and harmony to a world that has literally gone to hell in a handbasket. I believe the United Nations will begin uplifting him as the leader who speaks for all nations. Prophetically, he will not gain control over the world until midway through the Tribulation. Leading up to that point, any nations or leaders opposing his global influence (or attempting to make war with him) will likely be taken out by the rest of the international community. Eventually, all the nations and peoples of the world will have no choice but to pledge their allegiance to the Antichrist - or they will suffer the consequences, which will be deadly.

"THROUGH HIS POLICY HE SHALL CAUSE CRAFT (DECEIT) TO PROSPER IN HIS HAND; AND HE SHALL MAGNIFY HIMSELF IN HIS HEART, AND BY PEACE SHALL DESTROY MANY: HE SHALL STAND UP AGAINST THE PRINCE OF PRINCES (JESUS CHRIST); BUT SHALL BE BROKEN WITHOUT HAND." - DANIEL 8:25

In this verse, Daniel says, "by peace he shall destroy many." This could mean that he will spread the narrative that world peace can only be attained and realized through his leadership, and any nation, leader, or person who dares disagree, will be destroyed in the name of "keeping the peace." Next, the third seal is opened, and will release the rider on the **BLACK HORSE**. He will bring historic famine unto the earth -

"AND WHEN HE HAD OPENED THE THIRD SEAL, I HEARD THE THIRD BEAST SAY, COME AND SEE. I BEHELD, AND LO A BLACK HORSE; AND HE THAT SAT ON HIM HAD A PAIR OF BALANCES IN HIS HAND. AND I HEARD A VOICE IN THE MIDST OF THE FOUR BEASTS SAY, A MEASURE OF WHEAT FOR A PENNY, AND THREE MEASURES OF BARLEY FOR A PENNY; AND SEE THOU HURT NOT THE OIL AND THE WINE." - REVELATION 6:5-6

There's no question that this horseman brings an unparalleled season of famine upon the earth. The prophet Jeremiah had used the color black to describe famine more than once. Also, the food scarcity is made clear when we read, "a measure of wheat for a penny, and three measures of barley for a penny." When John had penned these words, a penny was equivalent to a day's wages. So, it is going to cost working people a *full day's pay* just to purchase a loaf of bread for their families. One would be able to purchase more barley for the same price because it is lower in nutritional value and often fed to livestock. A pair of balances that this rider holds represents food rationing.

The oil and wine being untouched during the famine indicates that the rich will still live luxuriously, getting drunk and hoarding riches, during the period of economic collapse (which historically harms the poor far more than the rich). Eventually, the poor will be able to afford the finer things in life when Antichrist's Mark is given. If they accept his mark (6-6-6) in their right hands or in their foreheads, then they will be able to buy or sell whatever they desire. It is sad that many souls of the left behind, who may have been turning to the Christ their loved ones once served, will sell out the Lord in order to join the upper class of society. I pray that those of you reading this will not make that costly mistake.

The Biblical saying rings true in every generation: "Money is the root of all evil" (1st Timothy 6:10). Remember the words of Jesus, in the Gospels of Matthew (16:26), Mark (8:36), and Luke (9:25) - "For what shall it profit a man, if he shall gain the whole world, and lose his own soul?" Seven years is a very short period of time compared to eternity. Would you rather live it up here and now, while turning your back on the Lord, or will you shun lusts of the world so that you can spend eternity in mansions with your family in Heaven one day? Any momentary sacrifices on the earth can reap eternal blessings in the hereafter.

Trust me when I say to you, even during the Tribulation, the Lord knows those that are His; and He'll always provide for your every need. Resist the mark when it comes, which condemns your soul to Hell for eternity, and God will give you *His mark* - which will seal your soul in His Kingdom forevermore. All of you left behind during the Tribulation must prepare to be faced with tough and consequential choices, and it will help you to remember that every prophecy found in this book is going to come to pass. The most important prophecy of them all is that the Lord will return to destroy Antichrist, his False Prophet, and Satan in the end. Yes, in case you haven't read the back of the Good Book, JESUS WINS.

If you are on the side of YHWH and His Christ during the Tribulation, it may feel like you're losing; but remember that you are ultimately on the winning side. To use a boxing analogy, it is better to lose a few rounds right now than to be knocked out of Heaven at the end of the fight! So, stand firm, stay focused, and never stop looking ahead to Round 12.

Now, back to the horsemen… as the fourth seal is broken, the fourth and final horseman rides onto the scene. He'll be mounting the **PALE HORSE** -

"AND WHEN HE HAD OPENED THE FOURTH SEAL, I HEARD THE VOICE OF THE FOURTH BEAST SAY, COME AND SEE. AND I LOOKED, AND BEHOLD A PALE HORSE: AND HIS NAME THAT SAT ON HIM WAS DEATH, AND HELL FOLLOWED WITH HIM. AND POWER WAS GIVEN UNTO THEM OVER THE FOURTH PART OF THE EARTH, TO KILL WITH SWORD, AND WITH HUNGER, AND WITH DEATH, AND WITH THE BEASTS OF THE EARTH." - REVELATION 6:7-8

While the color of this horse is called "pale" in our English language, the Greek word used more accurately depicts a sickly green color. This color signifies pestilences or plagues that will be brought by the rider. It's unclear if there's only one horseman that is released by the opening of this fourth seal; because while the verse mentions one horse, it also says that Hell follows the rider known as Death. It is possible that they are both riding one horse; but even if they are riding separate horses, that doesn't change the fact they're working together to execute a singular seal judgment upon Planet Earth.

They will be responsible for taking the lives of 25% of the world's unbelievers, as the verse is clear that a quarter of Earth's population will be wiped out by the riders. According to today's global population estimates, this would be equivalent to roughly 2-BILLION human beings. I am sure some of you may wonder why I specifically said that "unbelievers" would be their victims. Am I implying that there are Christians on the earth? But didn't I make the argument in the Introduction that the Church would be raptured? The answer to both questions is *yes*. The believers on Earth at this time are those who came to faith in Christ following the Rapture of their loved ones. I hope that you who are reading this book are one of them!

I think that there will be many amongst the left behind who will pick up the Holy Bible for answers, or who will open a book like mine. This will lead to a new generation of Bible-believers on Earth, known as the "Tribulation saints." The main reason why I suspect only unbelievers will be affected by the sword, starvation, and the pestilences which Death will bring, is that the victims are then claimed by Hell. Hell was created for unbelievers. So, in this judgment, Death will take their physical bodies and Hell will then take their eternal souls.

Focusing on the specific methods that Death uses to claim its victims, I believe they all involve *pestilences*. Upon reading "the sword," I'm sure most of you would immediately think of combat weapons; but today, and more so during the Tribulation, some of the most dangerous weapons are biological and chemical. Both of these modern swords use infectious agents to incapacitate or kill the enemy. Next, Death uses "hunger." Starvation can leave the body susceptible to infectious diseases due to immunodeficiency. The last agent of pestilence employed by Death is "the beasts of the earth." Throughout history, most infectious disease outbreaks have been spread from country to country via animals.

While this chapter of Revelation certainly appears to be the worst tribulation that the world's ever seen, those were only four seals. There are still three more to be opened, which are followed by seven trumpet judgments and the seven bowls of God's wrath. Unfortunately, for unbelievers, the worst is yet to come.

JESUS SAID, TAKE HEED THAT NO MAN DECEIVE YOU. FOR MANY SHALL COME IN MY NAME, SAYING, I AM CHRIST; AND SHALL DECEIVE MANY. AND YE SHALL HEAR OF WARS AND RUMOURS OF WARS: SEE THAT YE BE NOT TROUBLED: FOR ALL THESE THINGS MUST COME TO PASS, BUT THE END IS NOT YET. NATION SHALL RISE AGAINST NATION, AND KINGDOM AGAINST KINGDOM: AND THERE SHALL BE FAMINES, AND PESTILENCES, AND EARTHQUAKES, IN DIVERS PLACES.

- MATTHEW 24:4-7

CHAPTER TWO

FIFTH AND SIXTH SEALS

AND WHEN HE HAD OPENED THE FIFTH SEAL, I SAW UNDER
THE ALTAR THE SOULS OF THEM THAT WERE SLAIN FOR THE
WORD OF GOD, AND FOR THE TESTIMONY WHICH THEY HELD:
AND THEY CRIED WITH A LOUD VOICE, SAYING, HOW LONG,
O LORD, HOLY AND TRUE, DOST THOU NOT JUDGE AND
AVENGE OUR BLOOD ON THEM THAT DWELL ON THE EARTH?

- REVELATION 6:9-10

THE FIFTH SEAL BEING opened has generally been interpreted
in one of two ways - either as a picture of Christian persecution
ramping up on Earth, or picture of previously martyred believers
crying out for the LORD's vengeance upon a Godless world that
persecuted and murdered them. I hold to the second view, and I'll
give my reasons in a few moments. Before I do, I want to explain
how the first view could come to pass if it were true...

During the Tribulation, specifically in the second half of this
period, Christians will be martyred for their Faith. In the previous
chapter, I talked about how people will still be coming to Christ
after the Rapture; and a big reason for this is that the devout loved
ones of those left behind talked an awful lot about being taken up
alive into Heaven in the years leading up to their disappearance. I
envision this inspiring the left behind to search for answers in the

Holy Bible, or in books like this one that were given to them for such a time as this.

Another reason is that the coming 144,000 Messianic Jewish Evangelists and the Two Witnesses will spark the greatest revival in history! Though, as of the opening of this seal, they've not yet arrived on the world scene. So, if the first view of interpreting the fifth seal's meaning is correct, then the Christians being martyred at this time are those who came to Christ through hearing about Him from raptured loved ones - or by Biblical materials given to them by family and friends. Since we know Antichrist won't start serious persecution of believers until mid-Tribulation, after Satan incarnates him, how and why would Christians be persecuted and martyred for their Faith this early in the game?

I think that it would be due to the chaos that grips the globe as a result of the first four seals being opened. This would likely lead to the Antichrist consolidating power on the earth and, while not yet being filled with the spirit of the devil, he would view the Christians as a hindrance to his agenda. Because of his deceptive appearance as a "peacemaker," and after recent wars, bloodshed, global famine, economic collapse, pestilences, and one-quarter of the earth's population being wiped out, I believe that the panicked world will begin looking to him to fix things. Since nations would be turning to him for answers and a solution, it would be a perfect opportunity for him to begin declaring war on Bible-believers.

Eventually, he'll make Christians, Jews, and Israel scapegoats for all of the LORD's judgments that befall this Godless world. Since I can't step into the future, I can't tell you exactly how he'll demonize them as the reason for all of the problems in the world - especially the famine, pestilences, and economic woes - but it will not be hard for him to do in a post-Christian world.

Examining history, we can see how Adolf Hitler was able to demonize the entire race of the Jewish people. He blamed them for everything that was wrong in the world and, sadly, much of the population he ruled over bought into the demonic lies he sold - hook, line, and sinker. If Hitler (in a predominantly "Christian" world) was able to demonize an entire group of people who were beloved to the God of our Bible, then how much easier will it be for Antichrist to do the exact same in a Biblically-hostile world?

Now, the main reason why I hold to the second view - that the believers alluded to at the opening of the fifth seal are those who were martyred *before* the Rapture - is because of specific wording in Revelation 6:9. It says the souls of them that "were" slain. In other translations, the words "had been" are used for "were." So, either way, it is obvious through the most accurate renderings of this verse that the martyred Christians are being referred to in the past-tense. They aren't being murdered en masse *now*, and are not described as being martyred in the *near* future. This just validates my view that Christian persecution under the Antichrist does not ramp up until the *Great* Tribulation - the last 3 ½ years.

Verse 11 of Chapter 6 says that "white robes were given unto every one of them; and it was said unto them, that they should rest yet for a little season, until their fellowservants also and their brethren, that should be killed as they were, should be fulfilled." This implies that widespread persecution is *coming,* but isn't here at the time of the fifth seal. Also, every single seal judgment thus far has been the LORD dealing with unbelievers of the earth. The Book of Revelation is about His long-overdue wrath being poured out upon a God-rejecting world. His children are certainly *not* the victims of that wrath.

While Christians and Jews suffer great persecution during the Tribulation period, it will not be God doing the persecuting - it'll be Antichrist and the Godless world. The fifth seal is by no means the LORD opening up a time of persecution for His flock; but it's instead the Lord opening the prayers of every martyred believer in history for Him to avenge them - and avenge them *He will.* The sixth seal being broken, and every judgment that follows, will be God's long-awaited answer to their prayers.

As I've already said, if you have become Christian during the Tribulation, you will be kept safe during the coming plagues and disasters set to befall the world. That is not to say that extremely tough times and life-threatening persecution are not coming your way, because they most definitely are. But rest assured that it will not come from the LORD, but rather from Satan and the world. If you do end up being martyred for Jesus, take heart in His promise that you will *reign with Him* in the near future (Revelation 20:4).

The next seal to be opened is the sixth, and it will unleash the first of three *great* earthquakes that will shake the world during the Tribulation. It will be followed by a cosmic upheaval the likes of which the world has never experienced -

"I BEHELD WHEN HE HAD OPENED THE SIXTH SEAL, AND, LO, THERE WAS A GREAT EARTHQUAKE; AND THE SUN BECAME BLACK AS SACKCLOTH OF HAIR, AND THE MOON BECAME AS BLOOD; AND THE STARS OF HEAVEN FELL UNTO THE EARTH, AS A FIG TREE CASTETH HER UNTIMELY FIGS, WHEN SHE IS SHAKEN OF A MIGHTY WIND. AND THE HEAVEN DEPARTED AS A SCROLL WHEN IT IS ROLLED TOGETHER; EVERY MOUNTAIN AND ISLAND WERE MOVED OUT OF THEIR PLACES. AND THE KINGS OF THE EARTH, AND GREAT MEN, RICH MEN, CHIEF CAPTAINS, MIGHTY MEN, AND EVERY BONDMAN, AND EVERY FREE MAN, HID THEMSELVES IN THE DENS AND IN THE ROCKS OF THE MOUNTAINS; AND SAID TO THE MOUNTAINS AND ROCKS, FALL ON US, AND HIDE US FROM THE FACE OF HIM THAT SITTETH ON THE THRONE, AND FROM THE WRATH OF THE LAMB." - REVELATION 6:12-16

While the judgments of God unleashed up to this point have gotten the attention of the inhabitants of the earth, to say the least, the events brought forth through the opening of the sixth seal will have mankind running and hiding in fear. A great earthquake will kick off a series of earth-altering and space-altering catastrophes. The quake, and calamities that follow, will be unprecedented; and will fulfill age-old prophecies heralding "the Day of the Lord."

"I WILL SHEW WONDERS IN THE HEAVENS AND IN THE EARTH, BLOOD, AND FIRE, AND PILLARS OF SMOKE. THE SUN SHALL BE TURNED INTO DARKNESS, AND THE MOON INTO BLOOD, BEFORE THE GREAT AND TERRIBLE DAY OF THE LORD COME. IT SHALL COME TO PASS, THAT WHOSOEVER SHALL CALL ON THE NAME OF THE LORD SHALL BE DELIVERED." - JOEL 2:30-32 & ACTS 2:20

This earthquake, and the two that will occur during the Great Tribulation will make all of the other quakes throughout history look like minor temblors. To paint a picture for you, all quakes up until this point have been like 20-foot waves of the ocean rolling ashore onto a beach; while the great earthquakes of Revelation, in comparison, will be like 2,000-foot *tsunamis* which engulf every visible thing in their path.

Next, the sun will be darkened and the moon will become as blood. The longest possible duration of a total solar eclipse is just over 7 and a half minutes. This black sun will have no time-limit. Until the event actually takes place, there is no way of telling how long it will last. And I am sure that everyone has been fascinated with blood moons whenever they rise in the night sky; but as with the earthquake and sun, this blood-red moon will be exceptional. Most blood moons that I've witnessed appear as a dark orange or even tan color, but the Tribulation moon will be the unmistakable color of *blood* red. So much so, that the inhabitants of earth will tremble with great fear.

The fear that grips the earth will only increase more and more throughout the course of the cosmic chaos that will occur. Verse 13 says that the stars of heaven will fall unto the earth. The stars will most likely be meteorites, asteroids, or comets. Any of these striking Earth can do irreparable damage. If a literal "star" were to ever fall and strike the earth, our planet would most likely be vaporized, and all life would be wiped out. Since we know from reading further in the Book of Revelation that God still has plans for Earth, I believe the falling stars prophesied will be of the three that I have mentioned.

"The heaven departed as a scroll when it is rolled together"... This phrase has baffled every theologian and prophecy expert ever since the first Christian read John's *Revelation*. The great teacher Chuck Missler said, "This is one of the most troubling verses of all, and it is the one that I take most literally." Just to lighten the mood, he also went on to explain it in the most honest and simple way that I have ever heard - "So, what does it mean? *I have no idea.*" I second his take on the matter. It'll definitely be something that no human being has ever witnessed or even fathomed. The heaven (sky) will be rolled up. Wow. It is impossible to imagine.

While there are Christian teachers out there who find it much easier to allegorize the verse, it's theologically irresponsible to do so. Like Chuck said, it appears it's meant to be taken *literally*. We take the earthquake and all of the events involving the sun, moon, and stars literally. Why should we view verse 14 any differently? If God said that He is going to roll up outer space, then I believe He'll do it. He's the Creator after all. If He says it can happen, it can - and will - happen. There are over a dozen verses throughout the Holy Bible referencing the LORD stretching out the heavens. Ultimately, if you stretch anything out enough, it is going to split apart or, as with elastic or a scroll, after stretching it out it'll roll back up upon itself when you release your grip on its ends.

King David, speaking through the Holy Spirit, said in Psalm 102:26, "The heavens shall wax old like a garment; as a vesture shall God change them, and they shall be changed." YHWH also says that, in the end, He'll create a *new* Heaven and a *new* Earth (Revelation 21:1). So, it's clear that the heavens and the earth will wax old and need to be made new. I believe that the rolling up of the heavens in Revelation 6 is the evidence that the Universe and Earth, as we've known them, are coming to their ends - *literally*. Because of these historic and fearful events in the heavens and on the earth, the heathen of the world will finally come to realize that there is a God Who is judging the planet.

Sadly, they do not repent. Even though they acknowledge that the LORD exists and is unleashing His long-promised wrath upon the wicked world, they refuse to turn to Him and serve Him. All of the Godless world leaders, politicians, military brass, and rich men retreat to the bunkers that they have built under mountains or inside caves. While the middle-class and poor unbelievers of the world *literally* crawl into dirty mountains and caves to hide from the Lord's wrath. They will then continue in their idolatrous ways by calling on the earth *itself* to hide them from God, as opposed to praying to the Creator of the earth to end His judgments. This just goes to show why most of the world's population will follow after the Antichrist.

The men of Earth will be looking for someone to save them *from* the Savior of the world. They will desperately seek a god to arise from *among them* who'll stand up to the LORD of Heaven. Now, just who do you think that could be? Lucifer is finally going to have his grand moment in the spotlight. Enter *the Beast*. He'll paint himself as a "loving and merciful" alternative to the "cruel and vengeful" God. Though all of us true believers know that it is most certainly the other way around.

FOR THE GREAT DAY OF HIS WRATH IS COME; AND WHO SHALL BE ABLE TO STAND?

- REVELATION 6:17

31

CHAPTER THREE

144,000 JEWISH EVANGELISTS SEALED

I SAW ANOTHER ANGEL ASCENDING FROM THE EAST, HAVING THE SEAL OF THE LIVING GOD: AND HE CRIED WITH A LOUD VOICE TO THE FOUR ANGELS, TO WHOM IT WAS GIVEN TO HURT THE EARTH AND THE SEA, SAYING, HURT NOT THE EARTH, NEITHER THE SEA, NOR THE TREES, TILL WE HAVE SEALED THE SERVANTS OF OUR GOD IN THEIR FOREHEADS. I HEARD THE NUMBER OF THEM WHICH WERE SEALED: AND THERE WERE SEALED AN HUNDRED AND FORTY AND FOUR THOUSAND OF ALL THE TRIBES OF THE CHILDREN OF ISRAEL.

- REVELATION 7:2-4

BEFORE THE SEVENTH SEAL is opened, there is a brief lull in the pouring out of God's judgments upon the earth. Even though the Christ-rejecting world deserves wrath, the LORD still extends His great arm of mercy toward the sinners of Earth. He will give them another chance to be saved and to inherit eternal life through His Son, Jesus, and will do this by sealing 144,000 Jews of the 12 Tribes of Israel with His Holy Spirit. They will preach the Gospel to the post-Rapture world.

Up until this point of the Tribulation, the Holy Spirit has been present on Earth - as He has since the beginning of the world; but His presence has not been as prevalent since the Church went up in the Rapture. That is why Antichrist has been rising to power, and will soon control the entire world system. The overwhelming influence of the Spirit on the earth, through billions of believers, had kept the arrival of the world's most wicked leader at bay -

"THE MYSTERY OF INIQUITY DOTH ALREADY WORK: ONLY HE WHO NOW LETTETH (HINDERS) WILL LET, UNTIL HE BE TAKEN OUT OF THE WAY. THEN SHALL THAT WICKED BE REVEALED, WHOM THE LORD SHALL CONSUME WITH THE SPIRIT OF HIS MOUTH, AND SHALL DESTROY WITH THE BRIGHTNESS OF HIS COMING." - 2ND THESSALONIANS 2:7-8

If you are left behind, then that wicked one has finally been revealed on the earth. Though his true Antichrist nature will not be made fully clear until he sits in the Holy Temple of Jerusalem and declares himself to *be God*. It's at that time when his demonic influences escalate into full-blown possession by none other than Satan himself. Much of the world, being Biblically-illiterate, will continue to follow after him and even worship him as a god. Due to such a huge lack of Biblical knowledge around the globe, most citizens of Earth will accept his mark and will be doomed to Hell. Thanks to God's gracious and merciful nature, not everyone will have to suffer that fate. The LORD will raise up a remnant of His people to preach the identity of the Messiah (Jesus) to the world.

This remnant will be 144,000 Spirit-filled Jews. They will not only be sealed with the Spirit, but they'll also be *marked* with the Father's Name (YHWH) on their foreheads (Revelation 14:1) - in contrast to Satan's mark, which Antichrist will institute. Bearing YHWH's mark, they won't be harmed by the coming judgments of the LORD. The mark of God will also protect them from the Antichrist. Some may be arrested, tortured, and even imprisoned, but God's mark will bring them Divine supernatural protection so that they cannot be killed by the Beast. It'll be like when Daniel's friends, Shadrach, Meshach, and Abednego, had been thrown into the fiery furnace in Babylon.

34

"NEBUCHADNEZZAR THE KING WAS ASTONISHED, AND ROSE UP IN HASTE, AND SPAKE, AND SAID UNTO HIS COUNSELLORS, DID NOT WE CAST THREE MEN BOUND INTO THE MIDST OF THE FIRE? THEY ANSWERED AND SAID UNTO THE KING, TRUE, O KING. HE ANSWERED AND SAID, LO, I SEE FOUR MEN LOOSE, WALKING IN THE MIDST OF THE FIRE, AND THEY HAVE NO HURT; AND THE FORM OF THE FOURTH IS LIKE THE SON OF GOD." - DANIEL 3:24-25

Just as Jesus protected servants of the LORD way back then in the furnace, so too will He ensure that no death will befall His 144,000 chosen evangelists.

Throughout Christian history, there have been cults who have taught that the 144,000 are not whom God has said that they are - which is Jews of the children of Israel. False Christian "religious" groups, such as Jehovah's Witnesses, have taught that the 144,000 will only be faithful members of *their* church. According to their website, there are over 8.5-million Jehovah's Witnesses globally. This means that 98% of them are *not* the chosen ones apparently. I really like how Dr. Harry A. Ironside had put it -

"WHENEVER I MEET PEOPLE WHO TELL ME THEY BELONG TO THE 144,000, I ALWAYS ASK, WHICH TRIBE? AND THEY ARE INVARIABLY PUT TO CONFUSION FOR WANT OF AN ANSWER."

Almighty God, throughout the Scriptures, always says what He means and means what He says. If He says that there's 7 or 12 of something, a Bible student would call Him a liar by saying that He "symbolically" meant 6 or 120. When God says there will be a literal "144,000 Jews" saved and sealed during the Tribulation, then there *will be* 144,000 JEWS saved and sealed! There will not be 144,001 sealed, and not 8.5-million. There will not be 144,000 Jehovah's Witnesses, Mormons, or Catholics sealed - only JEWS. That is what God said and that is what God meant. It's sloppy and irresponsible theology when you twist His Word to suit your own views. As I've said, YHWH handpicks 144,000 Jewish preachers from the 12 Tribes of *Israel*. He chooses 12,000 from each Tribe -

"OF THE TRIBE OF **JUDAH** WERE SEALED TWELVE THOUSAND. OF THE TRIBE OF **REUBEN** WERE SEALED TWELVE THOUSAND. OF THE TRIBE OF **GAD** WERE SEALED TWELVE THOUSAND. OF THE TRIBE OF **ASHER** WERE SEALED TWELVE THOUSAND. OF THE TRIBE OF **NAPHTALI** WERE SEALED TWELVE THOUSAND. OF THE TRIBE OF **MANASSEH** WERE SEALED TWELVE THOUSAND. OF THE TRIBE OF **SIMEON** WERE SEALED TWELVE THOUSAND. OF THE TRIBE OF **LEVI** WERE SEALED TWELVE THOUSAND. OF THE TRIBE OF **ISSACHAR** WERE SEALED TWELVE THOUSAND. OF THE TRIBE OF **ZEBULON** WERE SEALED TWELVE THOUSAND. OF THE TRIBE OF **JOSEPH** WERE SEALED TWELVE THOUSAND. OF THE TRIBE OF **BENJAMIN** WERE SEALED TWELVE THOUSAND" - REVELATION 7:5-8

Conspicuous by their absence in these verses are the Tribes of Dan and Ephraim, but there is a Biblical reason for their omission from the group of 144,000. It was through Dan that idolatry first entered the Land of Israel, and Ephraim too was guilty of idolatry. He was also responsible for a civil war that divided the Tribes of Israel. In Deuteronomy 29:20, the LORD said that the names of idolaters would be "blotted out." Though we'll see God's eternal faithfulness regarding his promises toward Jacob and his 12 sons, when the Tribes of Dan and Ephraim still inherit land during the Millenium. Their punishment for past sins is that they will not be sealed with the rest of their brethren, and neither of their Tribes are divinely protected during the Tribulation.

In Revelation's list of Tribes, Ephraim is replaced by Joseph (his father) and Dan is replaced by Levi. The fact that only Jews are preaching the Gospel of Jesus Christ to the world, at this time, is just more proof that the Church was raptured *pre*-Tribulation. If believers like myself were still on Earth, you know darn well that

I would be preaching the Gospel. Yet, thus far, we clearly see the Tribulation is devoid of Christian influence. This can only mean that the Church is long gone (in a good way).

A big reason why we know that the Body of Christ is gone at this time is because, up until the original formation of the Church, God's attention was always focused solely on His beloved Nation of Israel. The Jews were the center of His attention. Once the Church Age began, the LORD turned His attention to the Gentiles - in order to graft many of them into His Family Tree. Once the Church Age ends, God will again shift His attention back to His chosen people - the Jews and Israel. Notice how the 12 Tribes of Israel are center stage again, meaning that "the Church" is not!

"I WOULD NOT, BRETHREN, THAT YE SHOULD BE IGNORANT OF THIS MYSTERY, LEST YE SHOULD BE WISE IN YOUR OWN CONCEITS; THAT BLINDNESS IN PART IS HAPPENED TO ISRAEL, UNTIL THE FULNESS OF THE GENTILES BE COME IN. AND SO ALL ISRAEL SHALL BE SAVED: AS IT IS WRITTEN, THERE SHALL COME OUT OF SION THE DELIVERER, AND HE SHALL TURN AWAY UNGODLINESS FROM JACOB: FOR THIS IS MY COVENANT UNTO THEM, WHEN I SHALL TAKE AWAY THEIR SINS." - ROMANS 11:25-27

The fulness of the Gentile Christians has come in, the Church has been raptured, and many in Israel are finally being unblinded to recognize that our Lord Jesus was truly their Messiah all along. Compare the above verse to Revelation 14:1-5, and you'll see that the prophecy will be fulfilled during the Tribulation Hour *to a tee*. The Jews are once again God's chosen vessels to bring His Word to the world - and bring it *they will*. Believe it or not, the greatest revival in history occurs during the Tribulation! That may shock some, but it is precisely what the Bible says will happen. I love how Hal Lindsey puts it, "They'll be like 144,000 Billy Grahams turned loose at once!" They will save so many souls during their ministry that their disciples cannot even be numbered -

"I BEHELD, AND, LO, A GREAT MULTITUDE, WHICH NO MAN COULD NUMBER, OF ALL NATIONS, KINDREDS, PEOPLE, AND TONGUES, STOOD BEFORE THE THRONE, AND BEFORE THE LAMB, CLOTHED WITH WHITE ROBES, AND PALMS IN THEIR HANDS." - REVELATION 7:9

It just once again goes to show the loving and merciful nature of the LORD. Though the Tribulation was meant to be the final hour of judgment upon a world that long rejected Him and His Son, He still offers a second chance to be saved in the midst of it. To all of you reading this who've been left behind, whether Jew or Gentile, will you take advantage of it? It might well be the last opportunity you get, because the judgments that are coming will increasingly get worse. While it won't be easy to be a servant of Jesus as soon as Antichrist assumes total control over this world, just remember that serving only one of these men will bring you eternal life - and it is *not* the guy on the earth. So, choose wisely whom you will serve.

THESE ARE THEY WHICH CAME OUT OF GREAT TRIBULATION, AND HAVE WASHED THEIR ROBES, AND MADE THEM WHITE IN THE BLOOD OF THE LAMB.

- REVELATION 7:14

CHAPTER FOUR

SEVENTH SEAL AND FOUR TRUMPETS

AND THE SEVEN ANGELS WHICH HAD THE SEVEN TRUMPETS
PREPARED THEMSELVES TO SOUND.

- REVELATION 8:6

WHEN THE SEVENTH SEAL is opened, Revelation 8:1 tells us that there will be "silence in heaven about the space of half an hour." I believe this is because the angels, and saints alike, know that some of the worst judgments of the Tribulation are about to be poured out upon Planet Earth. The LORD has held back His most extreme wrath for thousands of years because of His endless mercy; but, because He is a just God Who abhors sin, it's always been inevitable that He would have to unleash it someday. And that day and great season of His wrath has finally come.

The silence in Heaven has been dubbed "the calm before the storm" by many Bible Prophecy teachers; and at the time that the seven angels of God begin to sound the seven trumpets, the storm will begin. I suspect that two of these angels will be Michael and Gabriel - who are both mentioned numerous times throughout the Bible. Another may be Raphael (mentioned in the extracanonical *Book of Tobit*). As to the identities of the other four angels, we'll only know for certain when we get to Heaven.

The first four judgments that the LORD brings upon the earth through the angels are referred to as judgments of "thirds." This is because they'll each destroy ⅓ of something. As the seven angels await the go-ahead from God to begin blowing the trumpets, there will be severe weather occurring all across the globe and another earthquake. Immediately after the brief but devastating precursors to the judgments have passed, the first angel sounds his trumpet.

FIRST TRUMPET

"THE FIRST ANGEL SOUNDED, AND THERE FOLLOWED HAIL AND FIRE MINGLED WITH BLOOD, AND THEY WERE CAST UPON THE EARTH: AND THE THIRD PART OF TREES WAS BURNT UP, AND ALL GREEN GRASS WAS BURNT UP." - REVELATION 8:7

The first "third" to be destroyed in these trumpet judgments is the earth's vegetation - the trees and grass. They will be burned by fire falling from the sky. This fire is preceded by (or accompanied by) hail, and is said to be mingled with blood. Fire mingled with blood? Right about now, many of you are probably saying, "That *must* be an allegory." From a standpoint of human understanding, the explanation seems most plausible. What we must remember is that we are talking about *God* here.

"HE DOES GREAT AND UNSEARCHABLE THINGS, MARVELLOUS THINGS WITHOUT NUMBER." - JOB 5:9

He is the God of wonders. He created the Universe, raised the dead, caused animals to speak, has rained down fire from Heaven in the past, and turned water into blood. *Nothing* is impossible for the LORD. He is GOD for God's sake! If the Holy Bible says that hail and fire will be mingled with blood, then that is *exactly* what is going to happen. There is no reason to try to allegorize it.

For the sake of laying out every possibility, I want to share what some other Bible Prophecy teachers believe that the hail and fire mingled with blood is all about. John MacArthur believes that it describes volcanic eruptions caused by the recent earthquakes. He theorizes the fire is fiery lava, and that steam and water being thrown into the sky from the eruptions could cause hail. He also thinks that the dust and gases which are released could make the waters appear blood red.

His last suggestion may relate to the judgment brought about by the second trumpet, which is upon "the sea," but it doesn't fit well with this first judgment. Blood is clearly falling *from the sky*. It isn't described as "looking like blood," but is said to be literal blood. I am not shooting down his entire theory though, as I am sure that erupting volcanoes may have some role to play in the judgments of the Tribulation. I just don't see it fitting here. For the record, I respect MacArthur. He is a bold faithful man of God, and a great teacher and preacher. I just disagree with him here.

Another Bible Prophecy expert whom I have greatly admired, and agree with on a lot, is Hal Lindsey. Long before *Left Behind* by Tim LaHaye, there was *The Late Great Planet Earth* by Hal. That best-seller's sold over 35-million copies since 1973. He has written great books since then, and I have been reading some of them in my research for this book. Hal theorizes that the hail and fire mingled with blood will be caused by a nuclear detonation.

He's big on nuclear weapons fulfilling Tribulation prophecies, and he has good reason to believe that nuclear weapons will play a major role in End Times prophecy; because there will obviously be nuclear war during the Great Tribulation. There are too many verses throughout the Bible that make this crystal clear. Though, I personally don't see them fitting this first trumpet prophecy.

As far as "hail and fire mingled with blood," I tend to agree with Chuck Missler. He believed that these words should be taken literally - as do I. The reason I agree with him is because taking the verse literally makes the most sense. I do not think that there is a need to twist the Scripture to make it mean what we want it to mean. On its surface, the judgment appears to be cosmic in nature - with objects falling from the heavens. Thus, I cannot support the volcano or nuclear bomb theories in this instance. MacArthur and Lindsey may be right, but I'm hoping that I won't be here to find out! I am sure they both feel the same. Hail, fire, and blood will fall from the sky. That's all I know!

SECOND TRUMPET

"AND THE SECOND ANGEL SOUNDED, AND AS IT WERE A GREAT MOUNTAIN BURNING WITH FIRE WAS CAST INTO THE SEA: AND THE THIRD PART OF THE SEA BECAME BLOOD; AND THE THIRD PART OF THE CREATURES WHICH WERE IN THE SEA, AND HAD LIFE, DIED; AND THE THIRD PART OF THE SHIPS WERE DESTROYED." - REVELATION 8:8-9

When the second angel sounds his trumpet, three more thirds are destroyed - ⅓ part of the sea, ⅓ part of creatures in the sea, and ⅓ part of the ships in the sea. This judgment fits the volcano theory much better than the first trumpet, but the problem is that it is said to destroy ⅓ of the ships. I can't see a few volcanoes doing that. So, like the previous judgment, I think this is a cosmic event. The "great mountain" could refer to a meteorite, an asteroid, or comet. Contaminants from a massive space rock could spread across the sea, killing creatures therein, causing the sea to turn to blood, and the massive size of it would ensure the capsizing and destruction of a third of the ships. To me, this theory makes the most sense.

I follow a simple guideline when studying Bible Prophecy - if something can be taken literally, then it is literal (no matter how far-fetched it sounds). While, if taking something literally doesn't make sense in the picture that God is trying to paint, then I search for symbolism. The Greek word used for "as it were" can mean "like." John could've been saying it was "like a great mountain." In other verses of Revelation, he makes clear whenever something is literal. So, I do not see this being a literal mountain. I also don't believe it to be a nuclear bomb like some teachers have suggested.

I said earlier that I respect Hal Lindsey, but it seems he really reaches sometimes to tie every judgment in Revelation to nuclear weapons. Again, I repeat that nuclear war will have a place in the Tribulation - just *not* in every single judgment. All of the trumpet judgments are clearly from the LORD of Heaven, and meted out by angels. They come *from heaven*, not the earth. Nuclear warfare involves devastation brought about by MEN - not God.

THIRD TRUMPET

"AND THE THIRD ANGEL SOUNDED, AND THERE FELL A GREAT STAR FROM HEAVEN, BURNING AS IT WERE A LAMP, AND IT FELL UPON THE THIRD PART OF THE RIVERS, AND UPON THE FOUNTAINS OF WATERS; AND THE NAME OF THE STAR IS CALLED WORMWOOD: AND THE THIRD PART OF THE WATERS BECAME WORMWOOD; AND MANY MEN DIED OF THE WATERS, BECAUSE THEY WERE MADE BITTER." - REVELATION 8:10-11

Like the first two trumpet judgments, I believe the third trumpet involves a meteor, asteroid, or comet, plummeting to the earth. It would be irresponsible of Prophecy teachers to explain it away as something else, because the description is identical to the sight of one of these objects falling from the heavens. To me, a "great star burning as a lamp" couldn't be any more clear. The "third" that is destroyed in this judgment will be a ⅓ part of the waters. While the last judgment referred to oceans, this judgment is alluding to all other bodies of water on the earth - the rivers, lakes, streams, ponds, wetlands, etc. The star called *Wormwood* will poison the earth's fresh water supply, making it bitter and undrinkable. This is why John says that many men will die of the water.

Wormwood is mentioned throughout the Old Testament as a bitter poisonous herb that causes affliction. At this time in history, it will bring a season of unrivaled affliction to the inhabitants of Earth. Since the dawn of mankind, humans have not been able to survive without water. It makes up at least 60% of our bodies, and every living cell inside of us depends on it to continue functioning properly. We can go more than three weeks without food, but the maximum time that we can go without water is generally between only 3-7 days.

About 97% of Earth's water is in the ocean, and the previous judgment polluted ⅓ of it with blood. Less than 3% of our water supply is freshwater, and only about 1% of that is accessible since most of it is trapped in glaciers and snowfields. On top of all this, freshwater is used to irrigate crops; and crop irrigation is vital in providing Earth's population with enough food. When ⅓ of our freshwater is poisoned, and we can only access 1% as it is, water will be more valuable than gold and famine will be widespread.

FOURTH TRUMPET

"AND THE FOURTH ANGEL SOUNDED, AND THE THIRD PART OF THE SUN WAS SMITTEN, AND THE THIRD PART OF THE MOON, AND THE THIRD PART OF THE STARS; SO AS THE THIRD PART OF THEM WAS DARKENED, AND THE DAY SHONE NOT

FOR A THIRD PART OF IT, AND THE NIGHT LIKEWISE." -
REVELATION 8:12

The fourth trumpet completes the judgments of thirds. This time, a ⅓ part of the sun, the moon, and the stars are all darkened. This will lead to shorter days, longer darker nights, and large drops in temperature. On some cloudy nights, and in major cities, the stars are already difficult to see in the night sky. This event will make them nearly invisible, and will have detrimental effects on Earth. Vegetation growth, animal behavior, flow of the oceans, and daily lifestyles of human beings would all be thrown out of whack.

The first four trumpets being sounded lead to major food and water shortages all over the world; and just when you would think that things couldn't get much worse for the world, the next three trumpets are heralded by three "woes." A woe is an exclamation of grief or distress over an impending doom or the wrath of God. Out of the nearly 100 times that the word is used in the Bible, this is the *only verse* that ever repeats it three times. That doesn't bode well for the inhabitants of Earth going forward.

I BEHELD, AND HEARD AN ANGEL FLYING THROUGH THE
MIDST OF HEAVEN, SAYING WITH A LOUD VOICE, WOE, WOE,
WOE, TO THE INHABITERS OF THE EARTH BY REASON OF THE
OTHER VOICES OF THE TRUMPET OF THE THREE ANGELS,
WHICH ARE YET TO SOUND!

- REVELATION 8:13

45

CHAPTER FIVE

FIFTH AND SIXTH TRUMPETS

THE FIFTH ANGEL SOUNDED, AND I SAW A STAR FALL FROM HEAVEN UNTO THE EARTH: AND TO HIM WAS GIVEN THE KEY OF THE BOTTOMLESS PIT. AND HE OPENED THE BOTTOMLESS PIT; AND THERE AROSE A SMOKE OUT OF THE PIT, AS THE SMOKE OF A GREAT FURNACE; AND THE SUN AND THE AIR WERE DARKENED BY REASON OF THE SMOKE OF THE PIT.

- REVELATION 9:1-2

AS THE FIFTH ANGEL sounds his trumpet, another star will fall from heaven, but this star isn't like the literal heavenly bodies that recently fell to the earth. This star's referred to as "him" and "he," so we know that this is an angel. There are generally two theories for the identity of this particular angel. One: It is a high-ranking angel who's given authority to open the bottomless pit (abyss), so that torment of the wicked can begin and hopefully lead them to repentance. Two: It's Lucifer (Satan), or even another fallen angel (demon). I am not too dogmatic one way or the other, because the arguments presented for both theories make a lot of sense.

The compelling reason that some Biblical scholars give as to why it will be a faithful angel of the LORD, as opposed to Satan, is that Revelation 20:1-3 shows a holy angel in possession of the pit's key. It will be used to bind Satan, and cast him into the pit. Obviously, if Lucifer were to be given the key of the same pit in

Chapter 9, it wouldn't make much sense that he would later bind and cast *himself* into the abyss. The only way it could be Satan who is given the key, at the sounding of the fifth trumpet, is if it is only given to him for a short season - and then given to another angel later on, at the conclusion of the Great Tribulation.

While the reason for it not being Satan was convincing and backed up scripturally, so too are reasons why it very well could be old Lucifer who will be given the key. The first reason is that he's described in the Bible as *falling from Heaven* (Isaiah 14:12, Ezekiel 28:17, Luke 10:18 & Revelation 12:7-9). Another reason is that the abyss is opened to release fallen angels (demons) who have been bound there for millennia (2nd Peter 2:4 and Jude 6), so it'd make sense their leader would be the one to release them.

I do not think that the identity of this particular angel is too important though, because the fifth trumpet judgment is primarily about *what will be released* from the opened pit - not the one who is doing the opening of it. And what he releases from that abyss should send shivers down the spine of every unbeliever. When he opens it, smoke arises out of it - "as the smoke of a great furnace" - and causes great darkness to come upon the earth. One-third of the sun had already been darkened as a result of the last trumpet blast, and now it will be virtually blotted out.

"AND THERE CAME OUT OF THE SMOKE LOCUSTS UPON THE EARTH: AND UNTO THEM WAS GIVEN POWER, AS SCORPIONS OF THE EARTH HAVE POWER. AND IT WAS COMMANDED THEM THAT THEY SHOULD NOT HURT THE GRASS OF THE EARTH, NEITHER ANY GREEN THING, NEITHER ANY TREE; BUT ONLY THOSE MEN WHICH HAVE NOT THE SEAL OF GOD IN THEIR FOREHEADS. AND TO THEM IT WAS GIVEN THAT THEY SHOULD NOT KILL THEM, BUT THAT THEY SHOULD BE TORMENTED FIVE MONTHS: AND THEIR TORMENT WAS AS THE TORMENT OF A SCORPION, WHEN HE STRIKETH A MAN. AND IN THOSE DAYS SHALL MEN SEEK DEATH, AND SHALL

NOT FIND IT; AND SHALL DESIRE TO DIE, AND DEATH SHALL
FLEE FROM THEM." - REVELATION 9:3-6

These are no ordinary locusts being described here for many reasons. They'll be an innumerable army of demons, who'll come forth out of the abyss like a swarm of locusts, and will be allowed to torment sinners with great pain for five straight months. Five months is the lifespan of actual locusts. Unlike real locusts, they will not touch any vegetation on Earth. They will also not touch the 144,000 evangelists who bear God's seal in their foreheads. I believe that Christians in the Tribulation, who were saved by their preaching, will also receive Divine protection from these demons; because the locusts are God's judgment. The LORD's judgments target unbelievers to lead them to repentance. Christians will only be harmed or martyred by *the world* (Antichrist's regime).

The torment which unbelievers on Earth experience, because of these demon locusts, will be similar to the pain of a scorpion's sting. The victim of a venomous sting from a scorpion will often roll on the ground in agony and foam at the mouth. On top of this, even if men attempt suicide, they will not be able to die. If they refuse to repent, then God will see to it that they suffer through the full duration of this torturous judgment.

"AND THE SHAPES OF THE LOCUSTS WERE LIKE UNTO HORSES PREPARED UNTO BATTLE; AND ON THEIR HEADS WERE AS IT WERE CROWNS LIKE GOLD, AND THEIR FACES WERE AS THE FACES OF MEN. AND THEY HAD HAIR AS THE HAIR OF WOMEN, AND THEIR TEETH WERE AS THE TEETH OF LIONS. AND THEY HAD BREASTPLATES, AS IT WERE BREASTPLATES OF IRON; AND THE SOUND OF THEIR WINGS WAS AS THE SOUND OF CHARIOTS OF MANY HORSES RUNNING TO BATTLE. THEY HAD TAILS LIKE UNTO SCORPIONS, AND THERE WERE STINGS IN THEIR TAILS: AND THEIR POWER WAS TO HURT MEN FIVE MONTHS." - REVELATION 9:7-10

The description of these demonic creatures that we are given by John makes clear that they are not literal locusts as we know them today. Throughout his detailed description, you'll find that John uses the words "were like" and "as it were" - meaning they were not literally the things that he was describing - but *like* them.

First, he said that they were like horses prepared for battle, so they will not be literal horses. Next, they have the appearance of crowns of gold on their heads - but not literal crowns. He says that their faces were like the faces of men, and that they had hair like that of women. Again, he is describing what he saw in terms that we would understand. So, they're not literal men and women. They are still creatures. They will have teeth like lions, and have protective armor like breastplates of war. This indicates that they will be invincible and cannot be destroyed. The earth will not be rid of them until their 5-month period is complete.

The sound of their wings sound like chariots of many horses running to battle, but they will not be literal chariots and horses. Though there have been some teachers who try to associate these demonic locusts with modern-day vehicles of war, I can think of too many reasons why this can't be the case. The final description of the locusts is the number one reason why they cannot be tanks or helicopters. John says that they have tails like scorpions, with stingers by which they harm and cause great pain to unbelievers of the earth. They are obviously a type of insect creature, for the fact that John could only reasonably describe them as locusts.

They'll be possessed by demons, but they will not be an army of literal demons walking around on the earth and attacking men. We know that demons inhabit both people and beasts, so it is not far-fetched to imagine them inhabiting the bodies of these locusts. Jesus had once cast demons out of a man and into pigs (Matthew 8:31-32, Mark 5:12-13 & Luke 8:32). In verse 11, we are told that "they had *a king* over them, which is the angel of the bottomless pit, whose name in the Hebrew tongue is Abaddon, but in Greek tongue hath his name Apollyon." From both languages, his name is translated as "the Destroyer."

This is not Satan, as old Lucifer was most likely the one who opened the pit. It is instead another high-ranking fallen angel who had been bound in the abyss. I suspect this to be the demon who's mentioned throughout the Bible (Exodus 12:23, Job 15:21, Psalm 17:4 and 1st Corinthians 10:10). Also, the Spirit placed a peculiar phrase in the Old Testament Book of Proverbs, in Chapter 30 and verse 27 - "The locusts have *no king.*" Since the Bible interprets the Bible, I believe He placed that odd verse there so that we'd be able to discern what is being described in the Book of Revelation are not literal locusts. Regular locusts have no king. Those being released from the abyss DO - and their king is a chief of demons. Obviously, then, those serving him would be demons.

"AND THE SIXTH ANGEL SOUNDED, AND I HEARD A VOICE FROM THE FOUR HORNS OF THE GOLDEN ALTAR WHICH IS BEFORE GOD, SAYING TO THE SIXTH ANGEL WHICH HAD THE TRUMPET, LOOSE THE FOUR ANGELS BOUND IN THE GREAT RIVER EUPHRATES. AND THE FOUR ANGELS WERE LOOSED, WHICH WERE PREPARED FOR AN HOUR, AND A DAY, AND A MONTH, AND A YEAR, FOR TO SLAY THE THIRD PART OF MEN."
- REVELATION 9:13-15

When the sixth angel sounds their trumpet, another group of destructive demons is released to slay ⅓ part of mankind. These four fallen angels were bound in the Euphrates River, which runs through modern Iraq, Syria, and Turkey. This river was once the eastern boundary of Israel, and it has existed from the beginning - back to the time of the Garden of Eden. Because this river runs right through three modern-day Islamic nations, which are filled with terrorists and murderous regimes, I would not be surprised if the demons possess leaders of these nations or local terror groups to make war on their ideological enemies nearby and abroad.

We know from the Book of Daniel that there are demons who influence and control specific nations, like the "Prince of Persia" (Daniel 10:13). If this is the case, and Iraq, Syria, and Turkey are influenced by three of these demons, then what nation would be influenced by the fourth? I assume it would be Iran, Saudi Arabia, or Kuwait - all located in the drainage basin area of the river. The river is closest to Iran. So, let's say that it's Iran (though this isn't a dogmatic conclusion). This means that demonic princes of Iraq, Turkey, Syria, and Iran will influence leaders of these nations to form a confederacy to make war on much of the world, or they'd influence terrorists in these nations to unleash attacks on a global scale. Either way, they'll ensure a third part of humanity is slain.

"THE NUMBER OF THE ARMY OF THE HORSEMEN WERE TWO HUNDRED THOUSAND THOUSAND: I HEARD THE NUMBER OF THEM. AND THUS I SAW THE HORSES IN THE VISION, AND THEM THAT SAT ON THEM, HAVING BREASTPLATES OF FIRE, AND OF JACINTH, AND BRIMSTONE: AND THE HEADS OF THE HORSES WERE AS THE HEADS OF LIONS; AND OUT OF THEIR MOUTHS ISSUED FIRE AND SMOKE AND BRIMSTONE. BY THESE THREE WAS THE THIRD PART OF MEN KILLED, BY THE FIRE, BY THE SMOKE, AND BY THE BRIMSTONE, WHICH ISSUED OUT OF THEIR MOUTHS. THEIR POWER IS IN THEIR MOUTH, AND THEIR TAILS: THEIR TAILS WERE LIKE UNTO SERPENTS, AND HAD HEADS, AND WITH THEM THEY DO HURT." - REVELATION 9:16-19

A popular view among many Bible Prophecy teachers is that this is not an army of nations bordering the Euphrates, as I have suggested, but rather communist China. Their reason is that China comes, along with other Asian nations, from the east (land of the rising sun) in Revelation 16:12. They are prophesied to cross over the great river Euphrates. Also, China possesses one of the largest militaries on the planet. So, it is only logical that they would be the best candidate for possessing a 200-million man army. While these teachers could be right, let me give my reasons why I don't think that China is present here...

While I do believe China will most likely be the leader of the kings described in Revelation 16:12, I do not see them being the army that is described in the sixth trumpet event. China will cross over the Euphrates *during* the Battle of Armageddon, in Chapter 16 - *not* in Chapter 9. Why would they cross over the same river twice? It doesn't make much sense. China does indeed possess a large enough army to make up 200-million combatants; but if this army really were China, why are the 200,000,000 *not* mentioned in Chapter 16? Also, why are those "kings of the rising sun" *not* mentioned here in Chapter 9?

The four demon princes from the Euphrates, like all demons, are most likely territorial. So, it is only logical they would inspire and influence nations closest to the Euphrates. China isn't that far to the east, but they are much farther off than the Middle Eastern nations I have mentioned. Also, nuclear weapons may be at play; and I think any nuclear war involving China will be a World War, and Armageddon is exactly that. Though there are some teachers who try to lump Chapter 9 with Chapter 16 and Armageddon, like with China, I've got reasons why I do not believe this is the case.

First off, Armageddon involves *all nations* of this world; and the battle will be fought in and around Israel. Here, we're talking about armies in the area of the Euphrates; and there is absolutely no mention of them coming against Israel. Next, we have not read any mention of the third Temple, nor of the Two Witnesses, as of yet. Third, the Antichrist has not yet assumed total control of the world with help of his False Prophet. Finally, Babylon the Great has yet to fall. All these things must occur before the final battle, and none of the above has occurred up to this point. Antichrist is likely involved in this campaign of the 200-million-man army that wreaks havoc on the earth, and I'll explain why in just a second.

Before I do, I have one last theory of a few Prophecy teachers to refute. Some say Revelation 9 alludes to the Gog-Magog War of the Book of Ezekiel (Chapters 38-39). This can't be so because the leader of the battle is Russian, and is known as "Gog." With the great attention that the LORD paid to the Gog-Magog War in Ezekiel, it wouldn't make sense for there to be no mention of Gog in this Chapter of Revelation if the battle were mentioned here.

The only time the names Gog and Magog are ever mentioned in the Book is after the 1,000-year Millennial reign of Christ on Earth, when Satan gets to make one final stand before he's locked in the abyss (the pit) for eternity. I firmly believe the Gog-Magog War takes place pre-Tribulation and will follow the Psalm 83 War. I write extensively about these two battles in my first two books. Since I do not think they will take place during this Tribulation, I refer you to those books if you want to learn more about them.

Now, the reason why I had said that Antichrist would be one of the four leaders the Euphrates' demons influence is because I suspect that his seat of power will reside in ancient Babylon. For those who don't know, Babylon is in Iraq - one of the four nations I'd first mentioned. Prophetically, Babylon has to be rebuilt; and I explain why in the coming "Babylon the Great is Fallen" chapter. Since the coming chapter and its events involve him defiling the Temple, breaking Israel's Peace Treaty, becoming the dictator of a One-World-Government, and declaring war on Christians, Jews, and Israel, then him becoming possessed by a demon (or demons) in this Chapter makes perfect sense. It paves the way for Satan incarnating him in the future.

Thus far, I have explained the nations and peoples that I think the army of Revelation 9:16 will be made up of; and, now, let me explain why these are armies of men - not demons. There are only *four* demons that come forth out of the Euphrates, while the army is made up of *two hundred million*. So, it is clear that the demon princes are supernaturally leading the army, and are not the actual army itself that is making war.

Earlier in this book, I've cautioned against allegorizing things in Revelation as modern weapons of war; but, in the instance of the horses, I believe that's what John could be describing. He says that the heads of the horses were like the heads of lions, that fire and smoke and brimstone came out of their mouths, and that their tails were like unto serpents that had heads - with which they do hurt. To me, the first image that comes to mind is a military tank. The front side of many tanks could be viewed as resembling the *head of a lion*. Tanks issue *fire and smoke and brimstone*. And while I'm not aware if there are tanks that have long guns on both the front and back of the vehicles, most of them do have rotating turrets that turn the main gun to the rear of the tank. This would explain a *snake-like tail*. To me, for someone like John who could have never even imagined motor vehicles or tanks around 2,000 years ago, I think the vision that he saw very closely resembles a modern tank. Am I dogmatic in this theory about tanks or some other weapon being described here? Absolutely not. We will not know exactly what these things are that John had described until they are actually here.

I thank God that we Christians who are raptured will not be around to see if I'm right. As for those of you left behind, I just pray to God that reading the Bible and/or this book has led you to repent and give your life to Christ. Because if I am wrong, and the things that John described truly are *literal* horses, having heads of lions and tails of serpents, shooting fire and smoke and brimstone out of their mouths, you're gonna wish that they were tanks! God help you if I'm wrong.

John closes out Chapter 9 of Revelation by saying that men which were not killed by these plagues did *not repent* of their sins of idolatry, murder, sorcery (drug use or witchcraft), fornication, or thefts (Revelation 9:20-21). The heathen have got to be on the hardest drugs on the planet! How could they have witnessed, and experienced all the judgments that I've written about, and not yet believe in YHWH? How they won't turn to Him for forgiveness is beyond my comprehension. They *deserve* Hell; and the Beast that will take them there is about to rise.

AND I STOOD UPON THE SAND OF THE SEA, AND SAW A BEAST RISE UP OUT OF THE SEA, HAVING SEVEN HEADS AND TEN HORNS, AND UPON HIS HORNS TEN CROWNS, AND UPON HIS HEADS THE NAME OF BLASPHEMY.

- REVELATION 13:1

CHAPTER SIX

THE ANTICHRIST

WOE TO THE INHABITERS OF THE EARTH AND THE SEA! THE
DEVIL IS COME DOWN UNTO YOU, HAVING GREAT WRATH,
BECAUSE HE KNOWETH THAT HE HATH BUT A SHORT TIME.

- REVELATION 12:12

FOR THOSE FOLLOWING ALONG in the Book of Revelation,
you may notice that I've skipped over quite a few Chapters. The
reason for breaking from the chronological order of the Book is
because most events going forward are occurring simultaneously,
and I'd like to lay them out in the most accurate sequence. There
are many key events and players that make up the final 3 ½ years,
during which Jesus said, "there shall be *Great Tribulation*, such
as was not since the beginning of the world" (Matthew 24:21).
The Antichrist seizing global power and rule, alongside the False
Prophet, occurs at the same time the Two Witnesses appear on the
scene in Jerusalem. Since the prophets of God will be an irritating
thorn in Antichrist's side, I want to examine him first.

At this point in his political career, he will be incarnated by
the devil himself. His true colors will finally show for the entire
world to see. Sadly, since much of this world will be so lost and
detached from the LORD, they'll have no problem with who he is
about to become. Before I go further describing "the Beast" he is

becoming, I'll focus on his career up to this midway point of the Tribulation. He is first revealed to the world after the Rapture of the Church - not anytime before. This is because the restrainer of the pure evil that the Antichrist embodies must be "taken out of the way" (removed), and that restrainer would be the Holy Spirit. The Spirit indwells believers on Earth. So, when you remove us (living temples of the Spirit) from the scene, the influence of God's Spirit is removed. If He remained gone, then no one on the earth would ever be saved again. Every human being would be destined for Hell. That is why the LORD sends 144,000 Jewish evangelists, and the coming Two Witnesses, to bring the influence of His Spirit back to the earth. That's the reason why you who are left behind are reading this book. If the Spirit was not working on your soul, you would have trashed this book and anything having to do with the God of the Holy Bible. You didn't and you haven't. Thank His Spirit for that!

Immediately after the Rapture, there will be a radio silence, so to speak, of the Spirit. He will have no one to speak or preach through. This lack of a universal moral compass is what opens the door for the entrance of the Antichrist. The historic event of the Harpazo (Greek for "the Rapture") results in a sudden mysterious disappearance of millions (if not billions) of Christians globally. This causes widespread panic around the world, creating a perfect atmosphere for the charismatic leader to finally rise to power.

I explained in the "4 Horsemen of the Apocalypse" chapter that he enters the world scene as a "man of peace," and does what was long thought to be impossible - succeeds in brokering peace between Israel and her hostile neighbors. Since the mid-1970s, world leaders (specifically U.S. Presidents) have tried extremely hard - and have all failed - at achieving this goal. The number one reason for their failure has been that Islamic nations surrounding Israel have never truly wanted peace with the Jewish State. They have wanted Israel *gone*. That is why citizens of the world (and even most Israelis) will heap praise upon this man, because he'll finally deliver what no one else in history ever could - real peace.

"HE SHALL CONFIRM THE COVENANT WITH MANY (ISRAEL AND MUSLIM NATIONS OF THE MIDDLE EAST) FOR ONE WEEK (7 YEARS): AND IN THE MIDST OF THE WEEK (3 ½ YEARS) HE SHALL CAUSE THE SACRIFICE AND THE OBLATION (OF JEWS IN THEIR TEMPLE) TO CEASE, AND FOR THE OVERSPREADING OF ABOMINATIONS (DECLARES HIMSELF TO BE GOD IN THE HOLY TEMPLE, AND SETS UP HIS IMAGE IN THE HOLY OF HOLIES) HE SHALL MAKE IT DESOLATE." - DANIEL 9:27

As the verse above lays out in detail, it will not be a lasting peace. Antichrist will actually be the one to break the covenant, and turn the whole world against Israel. That was the devil's goal all along, and that is why he propped this false messiah up in the first place. Satan has always hated Jews, and especially the Jewish State. He'll lure them into a false sense of peace and security, and then pounce upon them like the vicious roaring lion that he is - attempting to tear them to pieces.

When the Antichrist first arrives in the world of politics as the smooth-talking visionary with all of the answers, it won't just be Israel that will admire him for bringing peace. It will be the entire world. He will likely come around not long after the Gog-Magog War, which I suspect precedes the Rapture. Since Israel's enemies will be demoralized after their failure to wipe the Jewish State off the map, and Israel will have war fatigue, I believe the political atmosphere will be ripe for the Beast to swoop in and broker the prophesied covenant of peace. I've written extensively about this Gog-Magog battle in my previous books. Take a few moments to read them if you have not already.

While Antichrist deceptively enters the Tribulation period as a peacemaker, most of his Biblical titles reveal his true nature. He is called the...

- King of fierce countenance (Daniel 8:23)
- Willful King (Daniel 11:36)
- Idol Shepherd (Zechariah 11:16-17)
- Man of Sin (2nd Thessalonians 2:3)
- Son of Perdition (2nd Thessalonians 2:3)
- Wicked One (2nd Thessalonians 2:8)
- Antichrist (1st John 2:18 & 22)
- The Beast (Book of Revelation)

Other titles are primarily found in the Book of Daniel. The Old Testament prophet had given the most detailed description of this wicked dictator, which is even more thorough than the Book of Revelation's account. In Chapters 7-8 of the Book of Daniel, the prophet refers to him by the name of the "Little Horn." Daniel was given a vision by the LORD of the final world empire on the earth. Like John does in Revelation, He uses "beast" to describe a One-World-Government (Daniel 7:23). Antichrist is "THE Beast" of the beast that has ten horns (10 kings), and he is the horn that will rise up after them (the "little horn") which will subdue three of those ten kings.

Both Daniel 7:21 and Revelation 13:7 reveal that he "makes war with the saints and will prevail against them." This is another reason why the Church is raptured *before* the Tribulation begins, because he is said to overcome and prevail against "the saints." Yet, Jesus said that "the gates of Hell *shall not prevail against His Church*" (Matthew 16:18). If Antichrist (who's the ambassador of Hell on Earth) is prevailing against believers, we know that they *cannot* be "the Church." These believers are "Tribulation saints" (post-Rapture converts) that he will be making war against.

In verse 25 of Chapter 7, Daniel tells us that this Antichrist will publicly blaspheme the LORD - "he shall speak great words against the Most High, and shall wear out the saints of the Most High." Revelation 13, verses 5 and 6, says "there was given unto him a mouth speaking great things and *blasphemies*; He opened his mouth in blasphemy *against God*, to blaspheme *His Name*, and His tabernacle, and them that dwell in Heaven (Angels, Old Testament saints, and the Church)."

Also, in verse 25 of Daniel 7, it is said that "he shall think to change times and laws: and they (Tribulation saints) will be given into his hand until a time and times and the dividing of time." When Daniel says, "time and times and the dividing of time," it's his way of saying "three and a half years." This will be the second half of the Tribulation, during which the Antichrist begins his rule as dictator of a New World Order. This time frame is referenced in Revelation 13:5 (42 months = 3 ½ years). As to the changing of times, I believe that this means he will change the calendar in order to wipe connection to the life of Christ (BC & AD) from it.

He will also change laws - most likely moral laws inspired by God's Biblical Law. Daniel 8:12 says "he will cast down *the truth* to the ground." Doing Satan's bidding, this evil man will attempt to scrub all memory of Judaism and Christianity from the earth. The Holy Bible will be banned. Christians and God-fearing Jews will be imprisoned, or even put to death, when discovered.

The religious leader that rises alongside him, who is known as the "False Prophet," will originally be a Christian leader (horns like a lamb) who has global influence (perhaps the Pope); but he will come under demonic influence. He turns His back on Jesus Christ and on the true God, and will use his power and influence to turn the hearts of the people away from the God of gods and toward Antichrist. He'll be the Beast's right-hand man. His main goal will be to usher in a One-World-Religion, to compliment the One-World-Government. He succeeds in bringing all religions of the world together as one, and their god will be Antichrist. Daniel has a lot more to say about *the Beast* in Chapter 8 -

"IN THE LATTER TIME OF THEIR KINGDOM, WHEN THE TRANSGRESSORS ARE COME TO THE FULL, A KING OF FIERCE COUNTENANCE, AND UNDERSTANDING DARK SENTENCES, SHALL STAND UP. HIS POWER SHALL BE MIGHTY, BUT NOT BY HIS OWN POWER: AND HE SHALL DESTROY WONDERFULLY, AND SHALL PROSPER, AND PRACTISE, AND SHALL DESTROY THE MIGHTY AND THE HOLY PEOPLE. THROUGH HIS POLICY HE SHALL CAUSE CRAFT TO PROSPER IN HIS HAND; AND HE SHALL MAGNIFY HIMSELF IN HIS HEART, AND BY PEACE SHALL DESTROY MANY: HE SHALL ALSO STAND UP AGAINST THE PRINCE OF PRINCES (JESUS CHRIST); BUT SHALL BE BROKEN WITHOUT HAND." - DANIEL 8:23-25

There are many signs that herald the Rapture and Tribulation, but there's a specific indicator for the rise of Antichrist and it will be one that'll be very easy for believers to recognize - "when the transgressors are come to the full." Though there has always been sin, since Adam and Eve, the time for the Beast's arrival will be ripe when sin blankets the earth. Lawlessness will be the norm, and those who live holy lives will be virtually impossible to find. That is why, as I write this, I think the Rapture could occur at any hour in the near future - because sin and unrepentant sinners have become mainstream, setting the stage for Antichrist.

When sin is absolutely everywhere you look, that is when this "king of fierce countenance" appears. The definition of "fierce" is harsh, cruel, and forceful. All these adjectives give us an insight into the personality of Antichrist. Though he will come into the world picture "peaceably" (Daniel 11:21 & 24), under the surface he'll have the makings of a harsh, cruel, and determined dictator who will eventually seize global power on account of these traits.

Next, we read that he'll "understand dark sentences." When I first began to study the Bible, I used to always assume this meant he would be comfortable associating with wicked people such as Satanists and Islamists. While this will actually be true, as he is at least one of these things (possibly both), that is not what the verse implies. It actually means he will understand "difficult questions and riddles." And, no, this does not mean that the Antichrist will be obsessed with quiz games. I believe that it means he will be an intellectual, whom much of the world will view as wiser than all other leaders on the earth. As I have said before, he will have an answer for seemingly every pressing problem facing the world - specifically the geopolitical issues of the Middle East.

When Daniel says that "his power shall be mighty, but not by his own power," this means that he receives power from Satan - who is the current ruler of *this* world. We know that God is the Ruler of the Universe; but ever since Adam ceded authority over the earth to Satan in the Garden, the devil has maintained control over the world. Jesus referred to Satan as "the ruler of this world" in John 12:31. The devil said that he would *give* the kingdoms of the world over to Jesus if our Lord would fall down and worship him in Matthew 4:8-10. Paul had called the devil "the god of this world" (2nd Corinthians 4:4), and "the prince of the power of the air" (Ephesians 2:2). John states clearly, in Revelation 13:4, that the power which the Beast receives is *from* "the dragon" (Satan).

In Daniel 8:24, the prophet reveals how successful Antichrist will be in battle. Any nations that threaten his kingdom will be destroyed. When Daniel says that he destroys the "holy people," this is referring to the Jews - the chosen people of YHWH. This man will be like the second coming of Adolf Hitler, but so much worse. While you'd think that it would be impossible for anyone to be more of a nightmare for the Jews than that demonic Nazi dictator, the Beast destroys *two-thirds* of the Jewish population on Earth! Under the influence of the devil, the Antichrist will be the worst anti-Semite in world history.

In Daniel 8:25, we read that he will obtain much of his power - and continue to grow in power - through deceit. Since the Bible will most likely be banned and illegal to possess midway through the Tribulation, when he finally shows his true colors, he will be able to deceive those dwelling on Earth to believe that the Jewish people are a cancer that must be eradicated. Sadly, like in Hitler's day, the Biblically-ignorant population will buy into whatever the Antichrist is selling.

He shall also be a very vain man, "magnifying himself in his heart," requiring (even demanding) praise and worship for all that he accomplishes. Daniel goes on to tell us that "by peace he shall destroy many." This makes more sense in the NASB translation of the Holy Bible - "he will destroy many *while they are at ease.*" So, when people (specifically Jews) are dwelling in peace, he will pounce like a destructive lion. The first 3 ½ years of his career will be spent trying to gain the trust of the Jewish State, leading them into a false sense of security. In the second 3 ½-year period, he will turn on them and become Israel's worst enemy.

Finally, Daniel tells us that because he will be so egotistical, puffed up in his pride, and feeling invincible, he'll actually stand up *against* the Lord Jesus Christ Himself. We also read about this in the Book of Revelation (19:19). In both prophetic Books, God makes clear that when Jesus returns to Earth to save Israel from certain destruction, He will defeat Antichrist and Satan so swiftly that if you were to blink you'd miss it! After millennia of losing to God, you would think that the devil would learn. Nope. He will keep trying to fight the LORD all the way up until the very end, and the end result will always be the same.

Some of Daniel's most thorough descriptions of Antichrist's characteristics and career are found in Chapter 11. While I have already quoted some verses from this Chapter already, there are some who believe that the majority of Daniel 11 actually refers to Antiochus Epiphanes - the Greek king of Syria who invaded and captured Jerusalem in 168 BC. There are good reasons for them to believe so, as he fulfilled many of Daniel's prophecies to a tee. Others believe half of Daniel's prophecies in this Chapter refer to

Antiochus (while also an allusion to the Antichrist), and the other half is about the Beast of Revelation. I hold to this second view.

It is impossible to deny that the anti-Semitic King Epiphanes committed abominable acts against the LORD, His Holy Temple, and His Jewish people. At the same time, I suspect that much of what Antiochus did will be repeated by Antichrist in the future. Just as the Beast will seem like a second coming of Adolf Hitler, I believe that he will also be a carbon copy of Epiphanes.

After capturing Jerusalem, King Antiochus marched into the Jewish Holy Temple, erected a statue of the Greek god Zeus, and sacrificed a pig on the Altar. It is said that he then sprinkled the blood of the animal over the Mercy Seat and Ark of the Covenant in the Holy of Holies. These acts of Epiphanes, and revolt of the Jewish Maccabees that followed, appear to be laid out in precise detail by Daniel in verses 21-35. Verses 36-45 seem to begin a new description of a future leader in "the time of the end" (verse 35), which would be Antichrist. Along with many reputable Bible Prophecy teachers, I believe that verses 21-35 are foreshadowing the Beast. Let me give you examples from these verses as to why. Daniel says that this wicked leader will...

- Be a **vile person**
- Come in **peaceably**
- Obtain **the kingdom** (of Israel) by flatteries
- Have a **league (covenant)** made with him
- Work **deceitfully**
- Do **mischief**
- Speak **lies**
- Set his heart against - have indignation against - and ally with those who forsake **the holy covenant**
- Pollute **the Sanctuary (Holy Temple)**
- Take away the **daily sacrifice** (of the Holy Temple)
- Place the **abomination of desolation** in the Temple

- **Corrupt** by flatteries
- Murder, burn, imprison, and spoil **Christians and Jews**

Compared with other prophecies of Antichrist, it's hard not to attribute these verses to the coming wicked one. Going forward, from verse 36 through verse 45, Daniel paints a perfect picture of the End Times Beast. He says that this evil king will...

- Do according to **his will** (as opposed to God's Will)
- **Exalt himself and magnify himself** above every god
- Speak marvellous things **against the God of gods**
- Prosper till the indignation (**tribulation**) be accomplished
- **Not regard the God** of his fathers
- Not regard the **desire of women** (a homosexual?)
- Honour a god whom **his fathers knew not (strange god)**
- Cause them (**Muslims?**) **to rule over many**
- **Divide the land** (of Israel) for gain
- **Overthrow** many countries
- Go forth with **great fury to destroy**

Given the descriptions I've listed, it is possible that Antichrist will be Islamic. Though, I don't think that he'll be a Muslim from birth. He will most likely be born a Christian or Jew and then turn his back on the Faith of his youth. I suspect that he'll eventually *become* a Muslim. There are too many indicators for the scenario in the above prophecies. For instance, he defiles the Holy Temple in Israel. Islamists had bulldozed and defiled remains of the first two Temples on Jerusalem's Temple Mount. He will also enslave, spoil, torture, imprison, murder, and *behead* Christians and Jews.

Read Revelation 20:4. What group of people, throughout the history of the world, has been the most notorious for consistently committing these cold-blooded attacks against believers? Answer: Muslims. Daniel goes on to say that he will blaspheme the LORD

God of gods and not regard the God of "his fathers" - meaning he was raised as a Christian or Jew? He will also honour a "strange god," and this means a "false god" in the Bible (like Baal/Allah). He'll cause followers of this strange god to rule over many. Could they be Muslims? Revelation 13:4 says the people who worship Antichrist will do so because they worship *the dragon* who gives him power. Reading Revelation 12, we know the dragon is Satan. Guess who else is Satan? ALLAH, Islam's god.

The name "Allah" is derived from *Baal*, the chief of the false gods in the Holy Bible and God's archenemy throughout the Old Testament. Because of this, many believe that Satan was Baal all along - as he wanted to be worshipped "as god" since before his fall. Lucifer wanted to "be like God" (Isaiah 14:12-14). Through Islam, he has acquired billions of followers who worship him as a god all over the world. We know Allah is Satan for many reasons. The Quran of Islam is the antithesis of the Bible. Everything that God says is good, Allah says is bad - and vice versa. The Quran denies the Deity of Jesus, and says Christians and Jews will be *destroyed* by Allah. How different from what our God teaches -

"WHO IS A LIAR BUT HE THAT DENIETH JESUS IS THE CHRIST? HE IS ANTICHRIST, THAT DENIETH THE FATHER AND THE SON." - 1ST JOHN 2:22

Islam has an End-Time messiah, whom they expect to appear on Earth in their scenario of the Last Days. Interestingly enough, their messiah-figure is prophesied to do everything Christianity's Antichrist is supposed to do! Here are a few examples -

❖ **The Mahdi (Islamic messiah)** arrives on a white horse. **Antichrist** arrives on a white horse.

❖ **The Mahdi** signs 7-year covenant of peace - breaks it.
Antichrist signs 7-year covenant of peace - breaks it.

❖ **The Mahdi** persecutes and beheads Christians and Jews.
Antichrist persecutes and beheads Christans and Jews.

❖ **The Mahdi** will seize Jerusalem and defile the Jewish Temple, planting a black flag on the site to claim it as the property of Islam - making it a seat of Islamic authority. **Antichrist** will seize Jerusalem and defile the Jewish Temple, erecting an image of himself therein and sitting upon the throne demanding to be worshipped as God.

❖ **The Mahdi** will change times and laws - doing away with Western Calendars (based on the life of Christ) and replacing them with the Islamic Calendar (based on the life of Muhammad); he will institute Islamic Shariah Law as the new Global Law.
Antichrist will change times and laws - doing away with Western Calendars (based on the life of Christ); he will remove any and all laws that are Bible-based and institute his own set of global laws.

❖ **The Mahdi** places a mark on the foreheads of all "true muslims" that they may enter Heaven.
Antichrist places a mark on the foreheads or right hands of those who worship him (condemning them to Hell).

These are striking similarities to say the least! Basically, in the Quran, Antichrist is a "good guy." That should tell you whose spirit was behind the penning of the Quran of Muhammad. It sure wasn't the Holy Spirit of our God! I will give you one guess as to whose spirit was behind it, and I'll also give you a hint - his name starts with an "S" and ends with "ATAN." Get the picture? Other possible reasons why Antichrist may become a Muslim, if he isn't one to begin with, are two of his titles in the Bible - "the King of Babylon" (Isaiah 14) and "the Assyrian" (Isaiah 10). These both refer to a leader of what are historically (and currently) Islamic lands in the Middle East.

During his final 3 ½-year reign over the earth, the Antichrist may actually set up his home base in ancient Babylon of Iraq. I'll explain more as to why I hold this view in the coming "Babylon the Great is Fallen" chapter. In the "Mark of the Beast" chapter, you will read why *the mark,* which Antichrist requires all citizens of the world to receive, could be Islamic in nature. While I am not dogmatic about him being a Muslim, it's undeniable that there are too many reasons why he could be. And I know that some may say, "but he exalts himself over *all gods,* so how could he worship Allah?" I suspect he may pass himself off as Allah "in the flesh," just as Jesus came down as our God (YHWH) in the flesh.

You cannot study Antichrist's life without recognizing that so much of what he will do is meant to imitate Christ in a mocking fashion. Along with his sidekick, the False Prophet, he performs many signs, wonders, and even "miracles" (Revelation 13:13-15). This would make most people believe he is a god in human flesh. One of the greatest miracles he performs is a fake resurrection, by which he deceives many and causes them to worship him as god. I say "fake" resurrection because there is only One who can raise the dead, and that is our Father in Heaven. Satan may be able to perform many miracles by the power that God has allowed him to possess, but he will never be able to resurrect anyone.

The event that causes people to believe that Antichrist comes back to life from the dead is found in Revelation 13:3, where John says he saw the Beast having "a deadly wound that was healed." While the description of this wound is *deadly,* it says nowhere in the Bible that the wound led to his death. "Deadly" can also mean "life-threatening." So this wound that he had received could have, and maybe even should have, killed him. I don't think that it will. Inhabitants of Earth will be deceived to think it does though. That is why they will follow after him with awe when he emerges from the hospital alive and well live on global television. Much of the world will shout for joy, with the words, "who is like unto the Beast? who is able to make war with him?!" They'll view him as an invincible leader. They will see him *as God.*

One other issue concerning Antichrist that I want to address is his origin. Where does he come from? What is his race? To be honest with you, *I have no idea.* There is no one who does. Those who are alive with me as I write this will never know, because he is not revealed on the world scene until after the Church has been raptured by Lord Jesus (2nd Thessalonians 2:6-8). However, the Bible does give us some hints about his origin. Daniel 9:26 says he comes from the people who "destroyed the city and sanctuary." This refers to the Holy City of Jerusalem and the Jewish Temple. The destruction of the City and Temple was carried about by the Romans in 70 AD. This leads many to believe that the Antichrist will come from Rome.

While that is a possibility, people forget the Roman Empire blanketed much of the world. So, he could be European (English, Spanish, French, Austrian, Swiss, Ukranian, Romanian, and so on and so on). He could also be African, Arabic, Greek, Hungarian, Albanian, Bulgarian, Bosnian, or even Jewish. Thus, I don't think we should waste time speculating about his nationality, or about a region he'll come from. As I have just proven, there are too many possibilities. All we know for sure is that this leader will rule over the entire world someday in the future. I don't think it will matter one bit where he was born or had dwelt beforehand.

The horrible things that we do know for certain about him are what should concern all of you who are left behind. Because, I'm not going to lie, some of you will be martyred for your faith if you're found to be Bible-believers. Professing belief in our Lord Jesus and Father YHWH, during the final half of the Tribulation, will make you *public enemy number one* in the government of the Beast. But take heart, because any and all momentary persecution and suffering on this earth will lead to an eternity of blessings in the coming *new* Earth. Therefore, stand firm in faith. Don't waver or ever deny the Lord. If you live faithfully for Him during these last 3 ½ years, then He will keep all of the faithful promises that He has made to you in His Word.

Believe you me, *nothing* could ever compare to the blessings that He has in store (1st Corinthians 2:9)! So, do not be deceived by the Antichrist - nor by his accomplice, who will be performing many miracles and great signs. The next chapter will prepare you, in advance, for all that his False Prophet is going to do.

I BEHELD ANOTHER BEAST COMING UP OUT OF THE EARTH;
HE HAD TWO HORNS LIKE A LAMB, AND SPAKE AS A DRAGON.

- REVELATION 13:11

CHAPTER SEVEN

THE FALSE PROPHET

AND HE EXERCISETH ALL THE POWER OF THE FIRST BEAST
BEFORE HIM, AND CAUSETH THE EARTH AND THEM WHICH
DWELL THEREIN TO WORSHIP THE FIRST BEAST, WHOSE
DEADLY WOUND WAS HEALED.

- REVELATION 13:12

DURING THE SECOND HALF of the Tribulation, the Antichrist
is going to have a partner in crime who's going to help propel him
to power over all kindreds, and tongues, and nations (REV 13:7).
John dubbed this deceitful character the False Prophet. He is also
referred to as "another beast" in verse 11 of Chapter 13, meaning
he will be just as blasphemous, crafty, and evil as his counterpart.
Verse 11 also says that he has "two horns like a lamb," but that he
speaks "as a dragon." I believe this means he will originally be a
Christan leader (lamb - Jesus) who turns his back on the Faith and
on the true God, submitting to Satan's will (dragon - the devil).

He will unify all faiths of the world together into one global
religion. They will all worship Antichrist as their god, as verse 12
says that he "causeth the earth and them which dwell therein to
worship the first beast." John reveals even more about this Satanic
religious leader in verses 13 through 15 -

"AND HE DOETH GREAT WONDERS, SO THAT HE MAKETH FIRE
COME DOWN FROM HEAVEN ON THE EARTH IN THE SIGHT OF
MEN, AND DECEIVETH THEM THAT DWELL ON THE EARTH BY
MEANS OF THOSE MIRACLES WHICH HE HAD POWER TO DO IN
THE SIGHT OF THE BEAST; SAYING TO THEM THAT DWELL ON
THE EARTH, THAT THEY SHOULD MAKE AN IMAGE TO THE
BEAST, WHICH HAD THE WOUND BY A SWORD, AND DID LIVE.
AND HE HAD POWER TO GIVE LIFE UNTO THE IMAGE OF THE
BEAST, THAT THE IMAGE OF THE BEAST SHOULD SPEAK, AND
CAUSE THAT AS MANY AS WOULD NOT WORSHIP THE IMAGE
OF THE BEAST SHOULD BE KILLED."

Like Antichrist, the False Prophet receives his authority and supernatural power from Satan. He will be able to imitate many of the wonders that, up until this time in history, were distinctly attributed to the LORD and His holy prophets. For instance, he'll "make fire come down from heaven." This is what Elijah did in 1st Kings 18 and 2nd Kings 1. Just as magicians of Pharaoh had duplicated many of the plagues that Moses wrought in Exodus, so too this man will duplicate much of what the Two Witnesses do.

The Witnesses will begin to turn the hearts of many in Israel and across the world back to God, through their preaching and the great signs and wonders they'll perform. Then, the False Prophet will turn many of those hearts back to the Antichrist by imitating whatever it is that they'd done. The one miracle that he will never be able to replicate, which is something that only God in Heaven has done or can do, is raising people from the dead. That is what the LORD does when his Witnesses are murdered in Jerusalem.

After Antichrist, the False Prophet, and much of this Godless world spend three days actually *celebrating* the deaths of the two holy men - who will be widely viewed as false prophets, because Antichrist's accomplice duplicates their wonders - the inhabitants of the earth will tremble in fear and finally believe in the LORD when the Witnesses rise to their feet alive, and ascend to Heaven *live* on every television news network! Since this miracle does not take place until near the end of the Tribulation, the Antichrist and False Prophet will lead millions astray. They will commit many blasphemous acts against God for over three years straight.

The False Prophet uses his spiritual influence over the world to cause them to worship an image of Antichrist, which he will place in the Holy of Holies inside of Jerusalem's Temple. We are told that he has power to "give life" unto the image so that it may "speak." Throughout human history, this has been unimaginable. In our age of 3-D Artificial Intelligence, this has finally become possible. Refusal to worship the Beast and his image will carry a death sentence. This is another reason why I suspect Antichrist may be Islamic in nature, because there's only one *religion* on the earth that still murders those who do not conform - Islam.

In Revelation 13:16-18, John speaks of something that even non-Christians have speculated about for centuries - and that's the Mark of the Beast -

"AND HE CAUSETH ALL, BOTH SMALL AND GREAT, RICH AND POOR, FREE AND BOND, TO RECEIVE A MARK IN THEIR RIGHT HAND, OR IN THEIR FOREHEADS: AND THAT NO MAN MIGHT BUY OR SELL, SAVE HE THAT HAD THE MARK, OR THE NAME OF THE BEAST, OR THE NUMBER OF HIS NAME. HERE IS WISDOM. LET HIM THAT HATH UNDERSTANDING COUNT THE NUMBER OF THE BEAST: FOR IT IS THE NUMBER OF A MAN; AND HIS NUMBER IS SIX HUNDRED THREESCORE AND SIX."

6-6-6... The number's been synonymous with Satan in music, film, television series, the occult, and devil worship for thousands of years. Christians who despise and steer clear of everything that is associated with the number are widely mocked by the heathen. Meanwhile, God-haters embrace it as a form of rebellion against the LORD and Judeo-Christian tradition. There is finally a time coming when that number will be forced upon (or into) the hands, and/or foreheads, of virtually every human being on this earth.

When Antichrist rules the New World Order, the leader of his One-World-Religion will tell everyone on the earth that they must pledge allegiance to their one true "god" - the Beast; and that they must do so by accepting his *mark*, name, or number of his name (6-6-6), on or in their bodies. You have probably noticed I keep saying "in" the body when speaking of the mark, and I'll explain why in the next chapter which is all about the Mark of the Beast. No one on Earth will be able to buy or sell goods without it.

The rest of this chapter will probably seem controversial to a lot of people in the time that I am writing it. For those left behind, I think you will see it play out before your very eyes. I believe that the False Prophet will most likely be *the Pope* of the Roman Catholic Church. This is because he will originally be a Christan leader (two horns like a lamb) who holds global influence. While there are many denominations in Christianity today, there is no other "Church" in the world that has such a widespread presence in so many nations around the globe as the Catholic Church does.

I want to be clear that I am not saying Catholic brothers and sisters are not true Christians, or that their Church is evil; but as for the power structure of the Vatican, the Pope, and history of the Roman Catholic Church's leadership, it's been primed to be used by the devil during his hour of power on Planet Earth. I'll explain all the reasons why in the "Babylon the Great is Fallen" chapter. I strongly urge my Catholic family and friends to thoroughly read, study, and digest, everything that is in it. Because if you make the mistake of blindly following this Pope or your Church wherever *they decide* to lead you, you may just end up on the wrong side of Christ in the end. They have led millions astray before!

I believe the Pope is the top candidate for uniting all religions of the world under one banner because the current Pope (Francis) has already been attempting to do it. At an interfaith meeting on

February 4, 2019, he said, "Catholics, Muslims, and all believers (of all faiths) need to *unite*." He also said, "In the name of God, in order to safeguard peace, we need to enter together as *one family* into an ark which can sail the stormy seas of the world: the ark of *fraternity*." In my previous book, *Even More Signs of Our Times*, I shared this quote of Francis - "I belong to this religion, or to that one... it doesn't matter!" It matters Francis... more than anything!

Francis has also referred to the Holy Spirit as "the Apostle of Babel." If you know your Bible, then that should raise eyebrows. Babel is the location where Nimrod, the ancient Babylonian king, attempted to unite all people of the earth together as "one" - in a world where he would be their only king (like a god). That is why God confounded the language of Earth there, and had spread the inhabitants of this world out across the globe. Antichrist is often compared to Nimrod, because he will rule from ancient Babylon and unite the world under one government and one religion - of which he'll be *the god*. I find it interesting that *Mystery, Babylon the Great* is often identified as the Roman Church. Francis saying the Spirit is an "Apostle of Babel" adds credence to that theory.

Other reasons why I think this Biblically-illiterate Pope may be the False Prophet, or is paving the way for a future successor to be, is because he's said so many blasphemous things during his reign. Many of those things were recorded in my other books. In a nutshell, he has advocated for God-denying theories like the *Big Bang, evolution,* and *climate change* - he favors Israel's Islamic enemies over God's chosen Jewish Nation - he was the first Pope in history to allow reading of the Islamic Quran at the Vatican - he has said there is NO Hell - and has said that atheists will get to Heaven by "good deeds" (denying a need for salvation by Christ).

Finally, when Francis (Jorge Bergoglio) had been announced as the new Pope on global television, the exact time was 7:06 pm (Rome time) - which would be 66 minutes past 6:00 pm, or 6:66! If that's not an omen that all Christians should take notice of, then

I don't know what would be! There is no doubt in my mind that Francis is a false prophet. Only time will tell whether or not he is THE False Prophet. Thankfully, many Catholics don't support the liberal teachings of Pope Francis. The LORD knows the heart and intentions of His children, and so I believe many Catholics will be raptured with me in the Body of Christ.

Sadly, those who believe that the Pope's word *supersedes* the Word of God (as some Catholics do) will be left behind; because they give more credence to the traditions of men than to the Holy Bible. This is a very costly error. The Pope is referred to as *Vicar of Christ*, meaning "in place of Christ." Thus, there are millions (even billions) who follow him wholeheartedly, and do whatever he commands. I suspect this blind obedience will allow the Pope to inspire the remnant of the Church to pledge allegiance to the Antichrist - simply because he *commands* them to. Please heed my advice… If you ever want to reach Heaven at the end of the road, then follow God - NEVER MEN.

JESUS SAID UNTO THEM, TAKE HEED THAT NO MAN DECEIVE YOU. FOR MANY SHALL COME IN MY NAME, SAYING, I AM CHRIST; AND SHALL DECEIVE MANY.

- MATTHEW 24:4-5/MARK 13:5-6/LUKE 21:8

CHAPTER EIGHT

MARK OF THE BEAST

AND HE CAUSETH ALL, BOTH SMALL AND GREAT, RICH AND
POOR, FREE AND BOND, TO RECEIVE A MARK IN THEIR RIGHT
HAND, OR IN THEIR FOREHEADS: AND THAT NO MAN MIGHT
BUY OR SELL, SAVE HE THAT HAD THE MARK, OR THE NAME
OF THE BEAST, OR THE NUMBER OF HIS NAME.

- REVELATION 13:16-17

IF YOU'VE BEEN LEFT behind and the demonic (yet popular and charismatic) characters of the previous chapters have appeared on the scene, seizing global control, know that the infamous Mark of the Beast is coming soon. If the Bible and this book have led you to faith in Jesus as Savior and Lord during the Tribulation, please read this chapter thoroughly. By accepting the mark of Antichrist in your hand or your forehead, you will lose your salvation! You will not be entering Heaven at the end of the road. If I were you, I would consider riding out the remaining years of the Tribulation in hiding, or accept you will be martyred for your faith. These are your only two options.

If the mark hasn't been rolled out and mandated as of yet, I'd recommend that you stock up on all you need to survive for 3 ½ years. Load up on food, water, pet food, medicine, portable radios or televisions, batteries, and whatever else you think you'll need to survive. Without taking the mark on (or in) your body, you will not be able to buy or sell ANYTHING.

Before I get into details of this mark, I want you to consider one thing if you ever get so desperate as to entertain receiving it - Jesus is coming back down in just over three years. He is coming to destroy Antichrist, the False Prophet, and Satan. So, the earthly life that you preserve through accepting their mark will only buy you about 40 more months of lifebreath. After that, you'll have to spend eternity in Hell. If that sounds like a good tradeoff to you, then you need to have your head checked!

On the flipside, if you stand strong in your faith and refuse the mark, you'll spend eternity in God's Heaven which becomes the new Jerusalem. Will you choose 40 more months of living in this wicked world and then an eternity in fiery torment? Or does living with the possibility of martyrdom so you can spend eternity with your loved ones in Paradise sound better? This isn't a game show, but I would be choosing Door #2!

I believe this mark is just another way for the devil to imitate God. First, he will imitate the Holy Trinity - Satan in place of the Father, Antichrist in place of the Son, and the False Prophet in place of the Holy Spirit. Next, the Antichrist rides in on a white horse (as does Jesus) and masquerades as the "prince of peace" (which we all know to be Jesus). The False Prophet duplicates the miracles of God wrought by the Two Witnesses. Now, he and the Antichrist will force all citizens of the earth to take a mark of the name or number of the Beast in their foreheads or right hands - the *same* exact spots on the body that God has used to mark His faithful servants.

"THOU SHALT BIND THEM (COMMANDMENTS OF THE LORD) FOR A SIGN UPON THINE HAND, AND THEY SHALL BE AS FRONTLETS BETWEEN THINE EYES." - DEUTERONOMY 6:8

"AND THE LORD SAID, GO THROUGH THE MIDST OF THE CITY, THROUGH THE MIDST OF JERUSALEM, AND SET A MARK UPON THE FOREHEADS OF THE MEN THAT SIGH AND THAT CRY FOR ALL THE ABOMINATIONS THAT BE DONE IN THE MIDST THEREOF." - EZEKIEL 9:4

"THE ANGEL SAID, HURT NOT THE EARTH, NEITHER THE SEA, NOR THE TREES, TILL WE HAVE SEALED THE SERVANTS OF OUR GOD IN THEIR FOREHEADS." - REVELATION 7:3

"I LOOKED, AND, LO, A LAMB STOOD ON THE MOUNT SION, AND WITH HIM AN HUNDRED FORTY AND FOUR THOUSAND, HAVING HIS FATHER'S NAME WRITTEN IN THEIR FOREHEADS." - REVELATION 14:1

Since the devil has always wanted to be like God, he creates counterfeits for virtually everything associated with Him. He will even incarnate Antichrist in God's Holy Temple, in the Holy City of Jerusalem, and sit upon the Throne that has been prepared for Jesus. It is there, in the LORD's house, where he declares himself to *be God*. How brazen he will be against the Most High! All the while, the LORD laughs from Heaven - knowing Satan's time is short and running out.

Throughout history, we know that the mark of God given to the servants of the LORD has been either His *Name* (YHWH) or the *symbol* of the Cross (the Hebrew letter Taw). It's interesting to note that YaHWeH's name, in the Hebrew, resembles three sevens (777). So, His mark could be rendered a number, like Satan with the 6-6-6. Seven is the number of God, and it symbolizes holiness and perfection. Six is the number of man, and symbolizes sin and imperfection. Satan's mark will bear the *name* of the Beast, or his number. Since John mentioned the name and number apart from the mark itself, there may be an actual *symbol* (antithetical to the Cross) like a pentagram - serpent - or even an upside down cross.

In the world of Bible Prophecy, there are three widely held theories as to what this mark could be. **#1**: A barcode tattooed on the body, containing 6-6-6 in it. **#2**: Implantable microchip placed *inside* of the body bearing the name or number of the Beast. This is why I emphasize "in" when I speak of the location of the mark, regarding the forehead or right hand. *King James* version Bible is regarded as one of the most accurate renderings of God's Word on the planet, and specifically uses "in" - never "on" the hand or forehead. This sounds like a microchip implanted underneath the skin. Given that we already put microchips in pets and are using biometrics at jobs, on our smartphones, or in the security systems of homes, this scenario for the mark seems the most plausible.

It would be the easiest to get average secular people on board with. All Antichrist and his False Prophet would have to do is say that the implanted mark will protect children so they will never be lost, detects or prevents disease, eliminates need for vaccines and shots, is a safeguard against terrorism, and makes lives easier by eliminating credit cards, cash, and membership cards. I would bet that every important piece of information in someone's life would be in the chip - health, financial, location, and more. Most people will love this for the convenience aspect alone. Don't fall for it!

Finally, there is theory **#3** as to what the mark will be. It, too, is a very convincing theory. A former Muslim turned Christian, Walid Shoebat, laid out the case that the mark is going to bear the name of the god of Islam, Allah. Shoebat is a former Palestinian terrorist who once tried to disprove the Bible to prove the Quran was the true Word of God. In his study of both books, the LORD revealed to him the error of his ways; and he actually discovered that the Holy Bible was the truth, and the Quran was the fraud.

Being born and raised as a Muslim, Walid knows the Arabic language like the back of his hand. After he'd studied an original manuscript of Revelation, he noticed something familiar that took him by surprise. When he'd read Revelation 13:18, regarding the number of the Beast, he'd discovered the Greek numerals which represented the number may not have been Greek at all; but rather Arabic. Upon reading the Greek rendering for 6-6-6, Shoebat saw an Arabic phrase which he was very familiar with -

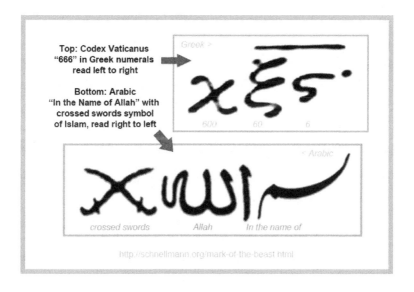

Top: Codex Vaticanus "666" in Greek numerals read left to right

Bottom: Arabic "In the Name of Allah" with crossed swords symbol of Islam, read right to left

http://schnellmann.org/mark-of-the-beast.html

When you take the middle character in the Arabic text, rotate it counter-clockwise, and then flip it in the opposite direction, you will find it aligns almost perfectly with the character resembling the letter "E" in the top image. The two other characters in both images are strikingly similar; and after comparing both texts, you would be hard-pressed to say there isn't some kind of connection. Walid suggests that the mark is not a literal 6-6-6 number, but is rather the Arabic phrase "*in the name of Allah.*" Given all of the connections of the Antichrist to Islam (documented in chapter 6), this theory sure makes a lot of sense.

There are some who will say that this theory cannot work, because John tells us to count the number. Since the above theory involves a phrase, and not a number, then it just doesn't fit the prophecy. This is when diligent Bible students must examine the original meaning of the text to verify or to invalidate this theory. Upon researching the definitions of the Greek words used for our English words "count" and "number," I came to find that Shoebat may be onto something.

According to *Strong's Bible Concordance*, the Greek used for "count" can mean "reckon" or "decide by voting." These words fit well with Walid's theory. As for the Greek used for "number," besides a literal number, it can also be defined as "a multitude" according to Strong's. With all this in mind, apply these alternate words to Revelation 13:18 and see if it helps or hurts his theory -

"HERE IS WISDOM. LET HIM THAT HATH UNDERSTANDING RECKON THE MULTITUDE OF THE BEAST: FOR IT IS THE MULTITUDE OF A MAN (MUHAMMAD); AND HIS MULTITUDE IS IN THE NAME OF ALLAH."

VERY INTERESTING to say the least. His theory actually holds up quite well, and causes us to view the Mark of the Beast in a whole new light. But, even after proving his theory has merit in verse 18, we still have to see if these definitions of the Greek hold up in the rest of the Chapter. Initially, it didn't appear to me that they would. When applying the word "multitude" to the word "number" in verse 17, it just did not make any sense whatsoever. How can anyone "have" the multitude of the Beast? They cannot. So, Walid's theory must be false then, right? Not so fast.

The key word that hurts his theory in verse 17 is "had." So, I referred back to Strong's for the alternate definitions of the Greek that was used in that verse. I discovered that "had" could also be interpreted as "hold fast to," or "be closely joined to." When we apply these alternate words in place of "had" we get -

"NO MAN MIGHT BUY OR SELL, SAVE HE THAT HELD FAST TO (WAS CLOSELY JOINED TO) THE MARK, OR THE NAME OF THE BEAST, OR THE MULTITUDE OF HIS NAME."

When inserting the alternate definitions of the Greek, Walid's theory is again validated as a great possibility. No one can "have" a multitude, but can certainly "be closely joined to" the multitude (followers of Allah - Muslims/Islamists). Believe it or not, Islam and Allah have *even more* connections to the Biblical Mark of the Beast. Walid has pointed to the fact that throughout the course of history, and up to today, Muslims wear badges bearing the words "in the name of Allah." The important thing for Bible believers to take notice of is *where* they are commanded to wear these badges on their bodies, in order to show their servitude to Allah. It just so happens that they specifically wear the badges on their *foreheads* and on their *right arms*!

All of these connections to the Mark of the Beast cannot be mere coincidence. On top of all of this, Revelation 13:1 states that nations who join with Antichrist have "the name of blasphemy" on their heads. Calling Allah "God" is blasphemy against the true God. Allah *denies* having a Son, and he commands Muslims to either convert or *murder* Christians and Jews - and specifically to behead them. Revelation 20:4 says Antichrist's regime *beheaded* those who had witnessed for Jesus and believed the Holy Bible.

The Divinity of Jesus Christ is denied in the religion of Islam, and He's viewed as a mere "prophet." Meanwhile, the warmonger pedophile Muhammad, the author of Islam, is portrayed as holier than Jesus. 1st John 2:22 says, "Who is a liar but he that denieth that Jesus is the Christ? He is antichrist, that denieth the Father and the Son." Allah and Muhammad deny Jesus is the Christ, and they also deny the Father-Son relationship described in the Bible. Therefore, they're ANTICHRISTS. Finally, the name "Allah" (as seen in the image I shared) is shaped like a *serpent*! Coincidence? I think not. One connection of Islam to Satan and his Antichrist could be written off as mere coincidence, but all the connections that I have recorded in this book form a *pattern*.

I'm convinced that Islam will be associated with Antichrist in some form or fashion. Am I dogmatic about this Islamic Mark of the Beast theory? No more dogmatic than I am about the other theories I've shared. My job as a Prophecy author is to lay out the possibilities. If anyone ever tells you that they know for sure what the mark will be, they are liars. They can't know. We *won't know* what it is for sure until it is here. I thank God that all of us devout Christians (in my lifetime) won't be around to find out! If you are left behind, then be wise and alert. Refuse *anything* being placed in your forehead or right hand by the government. Give your life to Jesus, and I promise that He will see you through until the very end. That is not just a promise... but a GUARANTEE.

IF ANY MAN WORSHIP THE BEAST AND HIS IMAGE, AND RECEIVE HIS MARK IN HIS FOREHEAD, OR IN HIS HAND, THE SAME SHALL DRINK OF THE WINE OF THE WRATH OF GOD, WHICH IS POURED OUT WITHOUT MIXTURE INTO THE CUP OF HIS INDIGNATION; AND HE SHALL BE TORMENTED WITH FIRE AND BRIMSTONE IN THE PRESENCE OF THE HOLY ANGELS, AND IN THE PRESENCE OF THE LAMB.

- REVELATION 14:9-10

CHAPTER NINE

THIRD TEMPLE AND TWO WITNESSES

AND THERE WAS GIVEN ME A REED LIKE UNTO A ROD: AND
THE ANGEL STOOD, SAYING, RISE, AND MEASURE THE TEMPLE
OF GOD, AND THE ALTAR, AND THEM THAT WORSHIP
THEREIN. BUT THE COURT WHICH IS WITHOUT THE TEMPLE
LEAVE OUT, AND MEASURE IT NOT; FOR IT IS GIVEN UNTO
THE GENTILES: AND THE HOLY CITY SHALL THEY TREAD
UNDER FOOT FORTY AND TWO MONTHS. AND I WILL GIVE
POWER UNTO MY TWO WITNESSES, AND THEY SHALL
PROPHESY A THOUSAND TWO HUNDRED AND THREESCORE
DAYS, CLOTHED IN SACKCLOTH.

- REVELATION 11:1-3

SPEAKING DIRECTLY TO THOSE who have been left behind,
you'll notice that the Holy Temple of the Jewish people has been
rebuilt in Israel. As I am writing this book before the Rapture has
occurred, I can only speculate how this prophecy will be fulfilled.
Currently, Islam's Dome of the Rock sits atop the ruins of the two
Biblical Holy Temples of the Jews. In order for the third Temple
to be built, the Islamic Dome must fall. You who are living during
the Tribulation know how that happened. Either I am going to be
wrong in my theory or you are about to say, "right on!"

I envision the Islamic Dome being destroyed in war between
Israel and her neighbors. A terror group on Israel's borders, such

as Hamas or Hezbollah, may accidentally blow it up with one of their own rockets - which they've constantly fired into the Nation of Israel for decades; or it may have been destroyed in an airstrike by one of the Jewish State's many regional enemies. If I'm right, you can personally give me kudos in about 3 ½ years!

I believe the construction of the third Temple may have begun shortly after Antichrist brokered the seven-year covenant of peace between Israel and her Islamic neighbors. If it hasn't been rebuilt, as of the time that those of you left behind are reading this, then mark my words that it *will be*. Prophecies of the Tribulation going forward involve the Temple of the Jews standing atop Jerusalem's Temple Mount. Antichrist will sit in that Temple, and in the Holy of Holies no less, demanding your worship. He will even declare himself to BE GOD -

"HE OPPOSETH AND EXALTETH HIMSELF ABOVE ALL THAT IS CALLED GOD, OR THAT IS WORSHIPPED; SO THAT HE AS GOD SITTETH IN THE TEMPLE OF GOD, SHEWING HIMSELF THAT HE IS GOD." - 2ND THESSALONIANS 2:3

I suspect that this could be the "abomination of desolation" that Jesus and the prophet Daniel both prophesied in Daniel 9:27, 11:31, 12:11, Matthew 24:15-16, Mark 13:14 and Luke 21:20-21. If this will not be that event, then it'll likely be when Antichrist's "image" is set up in the Temple by the False Prophet (Revelation 13:15). These Temple events are a turning point of the Tribulation period. They will begin to reveal the true nature of the Antichrist to those who have eyes to see. This is when times become very hard for Christians and Jews. Not due to the coming judgments of God, as those primarily target unbelievers, but because the devil is going to use Antichrist's global power system to make war on Bible-believers (Daniel 7:21 and Revelation 12:17).

The reason why the Beast is going to target Jews, along with Christans, is because the blasphemous acts that he commits in the

Temple will open the eyes of Israelis who fear YHWH God. They will no longer view him as a peace-making messiah, but rather as a Satanic blasphemer. This causes him to break the covenant of peace *"in the midst"* (middle) of seven years, which he brokered for them at the start of the Tribulation (Daniel 9:27). Coinciding with, or immediately following these events, the Two Witnesses of God will appear on the scene in the Holy City of Jerusalem -

"AND I WILL GIVE POWER UNTO MY TWO WITNESSES, AND THEY SHALL PROPHESY A THOUSAND TWO HUNDRED AND THREESCORE DAYS (3 ½ YEARS), CLOTHED IN SACKCLOTH. THESE ARE THE TWO OLIVE TREES, AND TWO CANDLESTICKS STANDING BEFORE THE GOD OF THE EARTH. IF ANY MAN WILL HURT THEM, FIRE PROCEEDETH OUT OF THEIR MOUTH, AND DEVOURETH THEIR ENEMIES: IF ANY MAN WILL HURT THEM, HE MUST IN THIS MANNER BE KILLED. THESE HAVE POWER TO SHUT HEAVEN, THAT IT RAIN NOT IN THE DAYS OF THEIR PROPHECY: AND HAVE POWER OVER WATERS TO TURN THEM TO BLOOD, TO SMITE THE EARTH WITH ALL PLAGUES, AS OFTEN AS THEY WILL." - REVELATION 11:3-6

These prophets of God will preach repentance and the Gospel throughout the final 3 ½ years of the Tribulation. Since they are prophets, they will most likely be revealing what is yet to come in the remainder of the Tribulation to those who'll listen. Obviously, for all those left behind who have Holy Bibles and/or this book in your hands, you already know what they will be preaching. Most will hear it for the first time. The Antichrist will loathe these men because they'll be exposing his Satanic nature to the world, but he won't be able to kill them. Like the 144,000, these holy men will receive a supernatural protection of God. No one and nothing will be able to harm them until their ministry is fully completed.

What will be amazing to see, to say the least, is they literally breathe fire upon their enemies. Anyone attempting to stop their preaching or hurt them will be devoured by fire. They are referred to as the *two olive trees* and *two candlesticks* because these are idioms from the Old Testament that infer they'll be continuously filled with the Spirit. Before I get into the miraculous powers that have been granted them by the LORD, I am sure everyone wants to know who exactly these witnesses are. I think I've got a pretty good idea, and most Prophecy scholars virtually all agree on the identity of one. The one name universally agreed upon is Elijah.

The first reason it could be Elijah is that he was one of only two men throughout the entire Bible who had never died, but was taken up to Heaven alive. Next, Malachi 4:5-6 says Elijah would be sent before the great and dreadful Day of the LORD. The Day of the LORD is the culmination of the Tribulation - the day when God unleashes the absolute worst of His wrath upon unrepentant sinners of the world and upon all of His enemies, especially Satan and the Antichrist.

The third reason is Elijah was the only Old Testament prophet who could call down the "fire of God" from Heaven (1st Kings 18:36-39). The Two Witnesses breathe fire. Reason number four is that he was the prophet at whose word the heavens "were shut" so it "rained not" for 3 ½ years (1st Kings 17:1 and James 5:17). This is another specific power these Two Witnesses will possess. Many Prophecy students are adamant that Elijah is one of the two because the heavens are shut and it rains not in the Tribulation for the exact same number of years as in Elijah's day - 3 ½ years.

So, since we have determined that Elijah is most likely one of the two, then who could the other be? There are two names most often suggested by theologians - Enoch or Moses. In my earliest years of Bible study, I believed Enoch was the other witness. The reason I came to that conclusion was because Enoch was the only other man in history who had never died, and was taken up into Heaven alive. It seemed like a pretty logical theory. The two men who never died, Elijah and Enoch, would come back down as the Two Witnesses. I have since changed my mind.

I now suspect Moses to be the other witness, and I have more than one reason for believing that - as opposed to just one reason for Enoch. There were two prophets of God in the Bible whose ministries were unfinished because they weren't fully obedient to God: Moses and Elijah. Elijah ran from Baal-worshipping Queen Jezebel in fear, and asked God to take his life. So, though he had started out a courageous man of God, he didn't finish running his race boldly. He instead cowered under pressure of persecution. I am sure that he has hoped for a second chance to end his life on the right note, and he will get it this time around.

When Moses was nearing the end of his life and ministry, he disobeyed a command of God because he was so aggravated with the children of Israel that he lashed out at them in a fit of anger. It was because of this act of disobedience, the man whose entire life was about leading the Israelites to their Promised Land would not be allowed to enter the Land himself. Yet another disappointing ending for a great prophet of the LORD. I would think that Moses is looking for a second chance to get it right as much as Elijah is. I believe that, like the Tishbite, he will get that chance.

Another convincing reason why the second witness could be Moses is that he is the prophet who smote Egypt with the plagues of the LORD and turned the waters to blood. These are the other two powers the witnesses are said to possess. Also, during Jesus' transfiguration on the Mount, His disciples witnessed Him speak to *two* specific men: MOSES and ELIJAH (Matthew 17:3, Mark 9:4, and Luke 9:30). Was this event a foreshadow? Of course, no one can be dogmatic about who these Two Witnesses are; because their names are not given. But I think God gave us enough clues to put two and two together (pun intended).

Some of you may ask, why two witnesses? Is there a specific Biblical meaning or reasoning for the number? Actually, there is.

God has always required the mouths of two witnesses for matters to be established as truth. Since two witnesses are symbolic of the *truth* being spoken, the LORD is hoping the devout Jews of Israel recognize this connection to their Law. While the 144,000 Jewish evangelists are preaching to the entire world, these two witnesses will be preaching strictly to Israel; because their feet do not leave Jerusalem until they are taken up to Heaven.

"AND WHEN THEY SHALL HAVE FINISHED THEIR TESTIMONY, THE BEAST THAT ASCENDETH OUT OF THE BOTTOMLESS PIT SHALL MAKE WAR AGAINST THEM, AND SHALL OVERCOME THEM, AND KILL THEM. THEIR DEAD BODIES SHALL LIE IN THE STREET OF THE GREAT CITY, WHICH SPIRITUALLY IS CALLED SODOM AND EGYPT, WHERE ALSO OUR LORD WAS CRUCIFIED. THEY OF THE PEOPLE AND KINDREDS AND TONGUES AND NATIONS SHALL SEE THEIR DEAD BODIES THREE DAYS AND AN HALF, AND SHALL NOT SUFFER THEIR DEAD BODIES TO BE PUT IN GRAVES. AND THEY THAT DWELL UPON THE EARTH SHALL REJOICE OVER THEM, AND MAKE MERRY, AND SHALL SEND GIFTS ONE TO ANOTHER; BECAUSE THESE TWO PROPHETS TORMENTED THEM THAT DWELT ON THE EARTH. AND AFTER THREE DAYS AND AN HALF THE SPIRIT OF LIFE FROM GOD ENTERED INTO THEM, AND THEY STOOD UPON THEIR FEET; AND GREAT FEAR FELL UPON THEM WHICH SAW THEM. AND THEY HEARD A GREAT VOICE FROM HEAVEN SAYING UNTO THEM, COME UP HITHER. AND THEY ASCENDED UP TO HEAVEN IN A CLOUD; AND THEIR ENEMIES BEHELD THEM. AND THE SAME HOUR WAS THERE A GREAT EARTHQUAKE, AND THE TENTH PART OF THE CITY FELL, AND IN THE EARTHQUAKE WERE SLAIN OF MEN SEVEN THOUSAND: AND THE REMNANT WERE AFFRIGHTED, AND GAVE GLORY TO THE GOD OF HEAVEN." - REVELATION 11:7-13

As soon as their ministry reaches completion, Antichrist (the Beast) will have them murdered. Their dead bodies shall lie in the streets of Jerusalem for 3 ½ days, and a majority of the world will actually *celebrate* their deaths, as the two prophets will be viewed as tormenting mankind. The Godless world does not want to hear about sin or repentance. It is like that as I pen this, in my day and age. So, I can only imagine how much more heathen of the earth will absolutely loathe Godly messages of "live holy" and "adhere to the Law of God" during the Great Tribulation.

While I believe they will minister solely to Israel, we're going to find going forward that these men are no strangers to the rest of the world. They'll be in the headlines of broadcast news networks across the globe, because of the supernatural powers they possess. This will draw great attention to them. If there's still social media after the Rapture, I bet they'll be called bigots, religious zealots, fire-breathing freaks, and crazy Christians. As to the Rapture, I'm sure governments of the world explained away the event as some alien abduction, consequences of leaked radiation (possibly from nuclear weapons used in the Gog-Magog War), or they'll say that it was due to "climate change" or "global warming."

Most secular-minded citizens of the earth won't attribute the mass disappearance of millions of Christians to the Rapture. The majority of the world will likely mock Bible-believers during the Tribulation just as much as they do in my day - and even more so. I would love to see the faces of those mockers of God and haters of Christians when the LORD revives the lifeless bodies of these witnesses on live TV. Antichrist will hate them so much that he will leave their dead bodies on the street where they perished in Jerusalem. Big mistake! While the world is celebrating the deaths of these pesky prophets, and newscasters and pundits are talking trash about them, imagine their reactions when these men of God rise to their feet 3 ½ days later - on live television!

While cameras are still rolling, they'll be taken up to Heaven for the entire world to see. This miraculous event will be followed by another great earthquake, which takes 7,000 lives and destroys 1/10 of Jerusalem. Believe it or not, after all of this, unbelievers of the world still refuse to repent and turn to God. There is good news though. After witnessing one-tenth of the Holy City being destroyed in the quake, many Israelis believe the preaching of the witnesses and accept Jesus as their Messiah and Lord. They will give glory to the God of Heaven. HalleluYah!

AND THE SEVENTH ANGEL SOUNDED; AND THERE WERE GREAT VOICES IN HEAVEN, SAYING, THE KINGDOMS OF THIS WORLD SHALL BECOME THE KINGDOMS OF OUR LORD, AND OF HIS CHRIST; AND HE SHALL REIGN FOR EVER AND EVER.

- REVELATION 11:15

CHAPTER TEN

7TH TRUMPET - 7 VIALS - 7 PLAGUES

AND I SAW ANOTHER SIGN IN HEAVEN, GREAT AND
MARVELLOUS, SEVEN ANGELS HAVING THE SEVEN LAST
PLAGUES; FOR IN THEM IS FILLED UP THE WRATH OF GOD.

- REVELATION 15:1

THE SOUNDING OF THE seventh angel's trumpet heralds the
unleashing of the third and final woe judgment of God upon the
earth. This woe will consist of yet another set of seven judgments
known as the seven vials (or seven bowls), and they contain seven
plagues that will be poured out upon Antichrist's kingdom. I have
always said that God's number is 777, and it is hard to argue this
when reading Revelation. In it, we read of 7 churches - 7 Spirits
(lamps) - 7 candlesticks - 7 stars - 7 angels - 7-year Tribulation -
7 seals - 7 horns - 7 eyes - 7 heads (kings) - 7 crowns - 7 trumpets
- 7 thunders - 7 vials - 7 plagues - and 7 mountains.

These are the major sets of seven in the Book, but I have also
discovered other instances where things are done in multiples of
seven throughout it. Upon diligent and thorough study, you'll find
that the number 7 is used nearly 900 times in the Holy Bible. Two
of the final groups of seven found within God's Word (vials and
plagues) are the culmination of His wrath that is poured out upon
a world that has long rejected Him and His Son.

The people who receive the absolute worst of that wrath have refused every chance given to repent, and are more than deserving of what will befall them. These immoral people don't even repent after they fall victim to the coming judgments! Instead, they curse and blaspheme the LORD. So, it is not that they disbelieve. They acknowledge God exists, but want absolutely nothing to do with Him or His holy ways and laws. Let's examine what the coming seven vials of seven plagues will be...

FIRST VIAL

"AND I HEARD A GREAT VOICE OUT OF THE TEMPLE SAYING TO THE SEVEN ANGELS, GO YOUR WAYS, AND POUR OUT THE VIALS OF THE WRATH OF GOD UPON THE EARTH. AND THE FIRST WENT, AND POURED OUT HIS VIAL UPON THE EARTH; AND THERE FELL A NOISOME AND GRIEVOUS SORE UPON THE MEN WHICH HAD THE MARK OF THE BEAST, AND UPON THEM WHICH WORSHIPPED HIS IMAGE." - REVELATION 16:1-2

For those that have been left behind, and who have come to faith in Christ Jesus as Lord, understand and take heart in the fact that *none* of these coming judgments will touch you. Not one! These plagues of God will be directed toward the unrepentant - all those "*which had the mark of the beast*" and "*them which worshipped his image.*" As I mentioned at the start of this chapter, these bowls of wrath are poured out specifically on Antichrist's kingdom and upon all those that have pledged allegiance to him.

The first vial being poured out brings painful sores upon them that had taken the Mark of the Beast upon their body. Since these sores are brought upon men by God, they will be incurable. There is no modern medicine or treatment that will be able to heal them. Once you have them, you'll be stuck with them for the remainder of the Tribulation. Imagine having a pain that even morphine will not numb! Agonizing screams will be heard across every street in the world. It will sound like Hell come to Earth.

In my last book, I wrote about how YHWH protects believers from His plagues and judgments in the same way He'd protected the Israelites when His plagues fell upon Pharaoh's kingdom. So, if you are one of the left behind who've become a Christian, God will keep the plagues from your body and your home. He will, in essence, *pass over* you. Just as the blood of a lamb on doorposts of the Jews in Egypt kept the plagues away from them, the Blood of the Lamb of God will keep every coming plague away from you! For *the Lord knows those that are His* (2nd Timothy 2:19).

SECOND VIAL

"AND THE SECOND ANGEL POURED OUT HIS VIAL UPON THE SEA; AND IT BECAME AS THE BLOOD OF A DEAD MAN: AND EVERY LIVING SOUL DIED IN THE SEA." - REVELATION 16:3

At first glance, this plague appears to be a repeat of the judgment from Revelation 8:8-9. It is not. In that second trumpet judgment, only ⅓ part of the sea had become blood and only ⅓ part of the creatures in the sea had died. In this vial judgment, the *entire* sea will become as blood and *every* living thing in the sea dies. The trumpets were a taste of God's indignation, and served as warning shots to the inhabitants of Earth. The vials being poured out now are the total manifestation of God's wrath.

THIRD VIAL

"AND THE THIRD ANGEL POURED OUT HIS VIAL UPON THE RIVERS AND FOUNTAINS OF WATERS; AND THEY BECAME BLOOD. AND I HEARD THE ANGEL OF THE WATERS SAY, THOU ART RIGHTEOUS, O LORD, WHICH ART, AND WAST, AND SHALT BE, BECAUSE THOU HAST JUDGED THUS. FOR THEY HAVE SHED THE BLOOD OF SAINTS AND PROPHETS, AND THOU HAST GIVEN THEM BLOOD TO DRINK; FOR THEY ARE WORTHY." - REVELATION 16:4-6

Like the previous vial, this is similar to Revelation 8:10-11. But, this time, *all* of the rivers and fountains of waters upon the earth are poisoned and become blood - as opposed to only ⅓ of them in the third trumpet judgment. This plague is an act of vengeance for all persecuted and murdered believers (both Jews and Christians) throughout history. Anyone who remains on the earth at this time, bearing the Mark, is a living representative of every anti-Semite and antichrist who had ever walked the earth. They are now going to reap God's judgment for the blood of His saints and prophets that was spilled from the beginning. Poetic justice indeed. They had shed the blood of those who feared the LORD, and now they have been given nothing but blood to drink.

While there was still a small amount of fresh drinking water left on the earth following the trumpet judgments, there will be *no more* from henceforth. Water is a necessity for any living being. Now, it is *all gone*. Imagine not being able to bathe anymore for the rest of your life. It's literally becoming Hell on Earth for those who have rejected the God of gods.

FOURTH VIAL

"AND THE FOURTH ANGEL POURED OUT HIS VIAL UPON THE SUN; AND POWER WAS GIVEN UNTO HIM TO SCORCH MEN WITH FIRE. AND MEN WERE SCORCHED WITH GREAT HEAT, AND BLASPHEMED THE NAME OF GOD, WHICH HATH POWER OVER THESE PLAGUES: AND THEY REPENTED NOT TO GIVE HIM GLORY." - REVELATION 16:8-9

The fourth angel brings the greatest heat wave mankind has ever experienced. In my day, there are millions of liberals in this world shouting about "man-made" global warming. I keep trying to tell them that they are wasting their time. What will they do when this day comes that the North Pole will be as hot as Tahiti?! The Old Testament prophet Malachi prophesied this, saying, "Behold, the day cometh, that shall *burn as an oven*; and all the proud, yea, and all that do wickedly, shall be stubble: and the day that cometh shall *burn them up*, saith the LORD of hosts" (Malachi 4:1).

To those left behind still living at this time, and who refused the Mark of the Beast, aren't you glad that you heeded my advice and steered clear of the mark?! To many, it might have seemed to be the safe and smart bet to preserve their earthly lives; but I bet they are deeply regretting it now! Think about it... first, they have these painful sores that won't go away... next, their water sources are polluted so they can't wash those sores... now, their sores are made more painful than ever before as they are exposed to record heat from the sun. They've made their bed, and now they're going to have to lie in it.

The point of the Book of Revelation, and the plagues therein, is to lead remaining sinners on Earth to repentance. It is more so a Book expressing God's great grace toward a world that does not love him in return, rather than a book of His judgment. He could easily wipe out the remaining population in one fell swoop of His

Almighty Hand. Instead, He gradually pours out plagues, hoping that some would repent and turn to Him for mercy. Unfortunately, as this chapter of Revelation proves, some are too far gone after the devil. After this fourth vial is poured out, we find that instead of repenting, men *blaspheme* the name of God. It is unbelievable. They deserve every bit of judgment that's coming, for there seems to be no hope for their souls.

FIFTH VIAL

"AND THE FIFTH ANGEL POURED OUT HIS VIAL UPON THE SEAT OF THE BEAST; AND HIS KINGDOM WAS FULL OF DARKNESS; AND THEY GNAWED THEIR TONGUES FOR PAIN, AND BLASPHEMED THE GOD OF HEAVEN BECAUSE OF THEIR PAINS AND THEIR SORES, AND REPENTED NOT OF THEIR DEEDS." - REVELATION 16:10-11

The fifth angel pours out his vial upon the literal kingdom of the Antichrist. Given all of the prophecies of the Beast ruling over a One-World-Government system, it is likely that the plague of this fifth vial will affect the entire world. When verse 10 says "the seat of the beast," it is referring to Antichrist's throne. I do not believe this means a literal throne though, but rather the Capital city from which he rules. Darkness will envelop Babylon, and it will spread across the globe. Country after country will become cloaked in a great darkness, and I suspect this judgment will be similar to the plague that befell Pharaoh's kingdom in Egypt -

"THE LORD SAID UNTO MOSES, STRETCH OUT THINE HAND TOWARD HEAVEN, THAT THERE MAY BE DARKNESS OVER THE LAND OF EGYPT, EVEN DARKNESS WHICH MAY BE FELT. AND MOSES STRETCHED FORTH HIS HAND TOWARD HEAVEN; AND THERE WAS A THICK DARKNESS IN ALL THE LAND OF EGYPT

FOR THREE DAYS: THEY SAW NOT ONE ANOTHER, NEITHER ROSE ANY FROM HIS PLACE FOR THREE DAYS: BUT ALL THE CHILDREN OF ISRAEL HAD LIGHT IN THEIR DWELLINGS." - EXODUS 10:21-23

While there are some who may view this plague as a reprieve from the greatest heat wave in history, I beg to differ. Because the darkness that came upon Egypt "could be felt." They couldn't see one another, nor could they leave their homes during the time of thick darkness. The Antichrist's followers will gnaw their tongues because of the excruciating pain they'll endure from the sores. So, I assume this darkness somehow increases their pain (as it could be *felt*); and there's nowhere they can turn for any kind of relief - as they can't set foot out of their homes. This plague of darkness could symbolize that any hope for souls remaining on Earth, who have not yet turned to Christ, is lost. Everyone who hasn't been saved up to this point will never be saved.

Verse 11, of Revelation 16, tells us they will *again* blaspheme God, instead of repenting and turning to Him for forgiveness and mercy. They've proven that, no matter what pains or troubles are brought upon them, they'll never turn to the LORD. They'll never stop sinning. They have made it clear that Antichrist is their god, and that they will never change.

SIXTH VIAL

"AND THE SIXTH ANGEL POURED OUT HIS VIAL UPON THE GREAT RIVER EUPHRATES; AND THE WATER THEREOF WAS DRIED UP, THAT THE WAY OF THE KINGS OF THE EAST MIGHT BE PREPARED. AND I SAW THREE UNCLEAN SPIRITS LIKE FROGS COME OUT OF THE MOUTH OF THE DRAGON, AND OUT OF THE MOUTH OF THE BEAST, AND OUT OF THE MOUTH OF THE FALSE PROPHET. FOR THEY ARE THE SPIRITS OF DEVILS,

WORKING MIRACLES, WHICH GO FORTH UNTO THE KINGS OF THE EARTH AND OF THE WHOLE WORLD, TO GATHER THEM TO THE BATTLE OF THAT GREAT DAY OF GOD ALMIGHTY. BEHOLD, I COME AS A THIEF. BLESSED IS HE THAT WATCHETH, AND KEEPETH HIS GARMENTS, LEST HE WALK NAKED, AND THEY SEE HIS SHAME. AND HE GATHERED THEM TOGETHER INTO A PLACE CALLED IN THE HEBREW TONGUE ARMAGEDDON." - REVELATION 16:12-16

The time has finally come for the battle of the great Day of the LORD, the battle of *Armageddon*. World War 3 is about to break out, and the vial that the sixth angel pours out makes a way for all nations of Earth to gather to the ancient bloody city of Megiddo in Israel's Jezreel Valley. The thing that will make this World War different from all those before it is that nations are not coming to fight each other in Megiddo. No, they are all gathering together to make war on one specific Nation: ISRAEL. The Euphrates river is dried up so the Oriental nations, and their large armies, can make their way toward the Jewish State on foot.

Verse 12 refers to Asian nations, like China and North Korea, because they are described as "kings of the east" (which can also be translated as "kings of the rising sun"). The demon spirits that proceed forth from the mouths of Satan (dragon), Antichrist (the Beast), and the False Prophet go forth to inspire all other nations of the world to come to destroy Israel. Eventually, virtually every nation of the world will converge at Megiddo. The unclean spirits like frogs that are sent to bring the nations together for the final battle in history are not actual frogs. John says that they are "like" frogs, and are also described as spirits. Therefore, we derive from this description that they are not meant to be viewed as literal.

Like frogs, the evil spirits jump from nation to nation under a cloak of darkness and croak an anti-Israel narrative into the ears of world leaders. Since they will be sent forth from the mouths of the unholy trinity, I suspect the "miracles" they perform will be things spoken by Antichrist and his False Prophet coming to pass before the eyes of the world. Satan speaks through his two wicked puppets to the planet's leaders, attempting to convince them that Israel is the sole reason for all of mankind's plagues and woes. Antichrist would then say that the Jews are *the problem*; and that if such and such a thing happens tomorrow, "then I speak as GOD and whatever I speak must be heeded to preserve lives on Earth."

I'm sure that he will say, in a global televised speech, that the Jewish State's deep connection to the God of the Holy Bible is the reason why the world hasn't been able to experience a lasting peace or prosperity. He'll blame all of the ills of the world on the Jews, Christians, and our "archaic, bigoted, and hateful" God. He will then say something along the lines of, "if I speak truth about this matter plaguing our world, then fire will fall from Heaven at this time tomorrow!" The spirits of devils will be given power by Satan to work this great wonder in the sight of all mankind. Upon witnessing what Antichrist prophesied come to pass, just the way he said it would, the nations will ally together with the common goal of wiping out their one common enemy: Israel.

In verse 15 of Revelation 16, Lord Jesus inserts a message of inspiration to those who have come to believe in Him during the Tribulation - but also a warning for those who have not. He lets you know that His return to Earth is coming soon, and that those watching and ready will soon be rewarded. On the other hand, all those not expecting Him will get the shock of their lifetimes.

Yes, for those who are left behind and looking forward to His return, the time draweth so very near. As I've always said to those looking forward to the Rapture event, I now say to those awaiting His return to Earth... keep looking up! Because as armies of the world come to that place known as Armageddon, with the hopes of destroying Israel, they have no idea they'll actually meet their *own* demise there at the hands of Israel's coming King!

SEVENTH VIAL

"AND THE SEVENTH ANGEL POURED OUT HIS VIAL INTO THE AIR; AND THERE CAME A GREAT VOICE OUT OF THE TEMPLE OF HEAVEN, FROM THE THRONE, SAYING, IT IS DONE. AND THERE WERE VOICES, AND THUNDERS, AND LIGHTNINGS; AND THERE WAS A GREAT EARTHQUAKE, SUCH AS WAS NOT SINCE MEN WERE UPON THE EARTH, SO MIGHTY AN EARTHQUAKE, AND SO GREAT. AND THE GREAT CITY WAS DIVIDED INTO THREE PARTS, AND THE CITIES OF THE NATIONS FELL: AND GREAT BABYLON CAME IN REMEMBRANCE BEFORE GOD, TO GIVE UNTO HER THE CUP OF THE WINE OF THE FIERCENESS OF HIS WRATH. AND EVERY ISLAND FLED AWAY, AND THE MOUNTAINS WERE NOT FOUND. AND THERE FELL UPON MEN A GREAT HAIL OUT OF HEAVEN, EVERY STONE ABOUT THE WEIGHT OF A TALENT: AND MEN BLASPHEMED GOD BECAUSE OF THE PLAGUE OF THE HAIL; FOR THE PLAGUE THEREOF WAS EXCEEDING GREAT." - REVELATION 16:17-21

The seventh angel, holding the final vial, pours it out into the air. This is, first and foremost, spiritually significant; because Satan is the "prince of the power of the air" (Ephesians 2:2). I believe this is God's way of saying that the devil's playtime on Earth is over, and that he will soon be judged alongside the Antichrist, the False Prophet, and all who took the mark. My take on this judgment is backed up by the voice that proceeds from Heaven after this vial is emptied, saying, *"It is done."* This is the final judgment upon Antichrist's kingdom and Satan's world. Christ is ready to make His descent back down to Earth to defeat Satan, and his worldly armies, once and for all.

When the angel will pour out his bowl of the LORD's wrath upon the earth's atmosphere, this will lead to thunders, lightnings, a *great earthquake*, and large hail. This quake will be the largest in the history of the world. There has never been another like it, and there never will be again. Many shudder when hearing about massive 8.0-9.0 magnitude quakes striking the earth, and causing devastating tsunamis. Just imagine what the first ever double-digit quake will do to Earth! We don't have to imagine, because God tells us in the following verses of Revelation 16.

The earthquake causes the cities of nations to fall, meaning nations of the world will basically be destroyed by this mammoth temblor. Every island will be moved out of its place or completely covered, and every mountain crumbles to the ground or is covered by floods of the greatest tsunamis mankind's ever witnessed. The Holy City, Jerusalem, will be divided into three parts - but not due to a judgment. Israel will be the only Nation on Earth whose land is *blessed* by the alterations from the earthquake! Believe it or not, the Middle East continent (the epicenter of the quake) may be the only one remaining on the map after the great shaking.

When I say that Jerusalem being divided into three parts is a blessing, my foundation for this belief can be found in Zechariah (Chapter 14 and verses 4-11). The prophet gives details about the things that occur during the Great Tribulation. This man of God (who wrote his prophecies before Christ made His first coming to the earth) actually prophesied about Antichrist (11:9), the nations coming against Israel and Jerusalem (12:1-9 & 13:8-9), the Battle of Armageddon, the great earthquake, and the Second Coming of Jesus Christ (Chapter 14).

Most of the heathen remaining on Earth after the earthquake will likely be killed by the large stones of hail that follow. Verse 21 tells us the hailstones will be "the weight of a talent." In John's days, a talent weighed about 100 pounds. Today, people often get frightened over baseball-sized hail, but the heaviest hailstone ever recorded was only two pounds. Imagine a hailstone that's the size and weight of ten bowling balls! You can forget about broken car windshields, as these stones of hail will leave cars more mangled than a destruction derby!

Those surviving these horrendous judgments not only refuse to repent, but they *again* blaspheme God - even *curse* Him. What gall. It is one thing to not acknowledge your Creator, or to choose not to believe in Him; but it is a whole 'nother impious thing to actually *curse* your Maker! Hell had been created for people like these. Before I close, some of you may have noticed that I didn't provide any commentary for the second half of Revelation 16:19 about "great Babylon." That's because the coming chapter will be all about the judgment and fall of *both* the literal and the spiritual *Babylon the Great.*

AND THERE CAME ONE OF THE SEVEN ANGELS WHICH HAD THE SEVEN VIALS, AND TALKED WITH ME, SAYING UNTO ME, COME HITHER; I WILL SHEW UNTO THEE THE JUDGMENT OF THE GREAT WHORE THAT SITTETH UPON MANY WATERS: WITH WHOM THE KINGS OF THE EARTH HAVE COMMITTED FORNICATION, AND THE INHABITANTS OF THE EARTH HAVE BEEN MADE DRUNK WITH THE WINE OF HER FORNICATION.

- REVELATION 17:1-2

CHAPTER ELEVEN

BABYLON THE GREAT IS FALLEN

I SAW A WOMAN SIT UPON A SCARLET COLOURED BEAST,
FULL OF NAMES OF BLASPHEMY, HAVING SEVEN HEADS AND
TEN HORNS. AND THE WOMAN WAS ARRAYED IN PURPLE AND
SCARLET COLOUR, AND DECKED WITH GOLD AND PRECIOUS
STONES AND PEARLS, HAVING A GOLDEN CUP IN HER HAND
FULL OF ABOMINATIONS AND FILTHINESS OF HER
FORNICATION: AND UPON HER FOREHEAD WAS A NAME
WRITTEN, MYSTERY, BABYLON THE GREAT, THE MOTHER OF
HARLOTS AND ABOMINATIONS OF THE EARTH.

- REVELATION 17:3-5

I HAVE SPOKEN A great deal about Babylon all throughout this book. That's because it is an essential piece of the Tribulation. It is the only city, besides Jerusalem, mentioned numerous times in Revelation. Babylon receiving long overdue judgment from God is so important that the LORD did not confine it to one sentence, one verse, one paragraph, or even one Chapter; but He took two Chapters and over 40 verses to detail the fall of Babylon. This is because from the earliest times of humanity on the earth it's been *both* the geographical and spiritual home of everything that stands in opposition to the true God of Heaven and Earth.

Mystery, Babylon the Great and the *great city of Babylon*, in Chapters 17-18 of Revelation, represent spiritual and literal cities.

The first Babylon is a false religious system, and the second is the city in which that religion will be headquartered. I believe literal Babylon, in the Middle East, will serve as the headquarters of the Antichrist. Before I go into detail about these latter-day Babylons, I want to present a brief history of the city that has given birth to all that has ever been anti-God in this world. It explains why God uses the name Babylon to describe the religion that'll eventually become the One-World-Religion of Antichrist, and why He uses the name to describe the city where that religion calls home.

There are about 300 references to Babylon all throughout the Holy Bible, and *none* of them are good. Babylon has always been representative of sin and rebellion against the God of gods. It was the Capital of the first Godless world dictator, Nimrod; and, as I have already said, I suspect it will also be the Capital of the final world dictator, the Antichrist. Nimrod's name means "rebel"; and the correct translation for Genesis 10:9 should read, "Nimrod the mighty hunter *in defiance of* the Lord." Babylon is where Nimrod gathered all people of Earth together to build the Tower of Babel.

All of the world's false religions have stemmed forth from the city, along with all pagan occult practices that've been ignorantly or willfully inserted into most world religions. Sexual immorality was widespread there. Babylon means "Gate of the gods." I think this title implies that it is the supernatural hot spot for the coming and going of demonic spirits (who are the false gods of the world - Allah/Baal, Bel, Molech, etc.). Scripture backs up my theory, as Revelation 9 says that demons were loosed from "the great river Euphrates." Babylon was built as a port town on the Euphrates. This could be where Satan's seat (worldly throne) is located, and where he sets up a literal throne when Antichrist rebuilds the city for his Capital.

For all of the above reasons, it makes sense that all religions worshipping deities other than YHWH would have originated in Babylon. The One-World-Religion, brought into existence by the

False Prophet, is likely birthed through *Mystery Babylon*. Believe it or not, this spiritual Babylon will be rooted in Christianity. But it will turn its back on the true God. It then unites all religions of the world together to worship Antichrist *as God*. That is why we are going to find that this mysterious "woman" is referred to as a whore and harlot, as both titles symbolize spiritual infidelity. Just who is this woman? Will she always remain a *mystery*? Is there any way we can know her identity today? I believe that we can.

After examining all that John reveals about her in Chapter 17, which I will break down verse-by-verse, it is hard to deny that she sounds a lot like the most powerful global denomination in all of Christianity - the *Roman Catholic Church*. Now, before I go any further, I want to be clear about a few things. #1: We won't know for certain exactly who she is until the rise of Antichrist and his False Prophet during the Great Tribulation. Until then, any theory that I or other Prophecy teachers present is mere speculation. #2: I'm not anti-Catholic, and this isn't an attack on those practicing Catholicism. There are many in my family who are Catholics, and I was a practicing Catholic for the first two decades of my life.

Whenever I say that the Catholic Church is Mystery Babylon, understand that I'm referring to the power structure of the Church (Holy See, the Vatican, and corrupt top brass). I am not referring to local churches, priests, or parishioners. I've had friends that are Catholic priests and deacons, and I do not believe that they have the slightest idea about the kinds of shameful things the leaders of their Church have done, are doing, or will do, which I'm going to lay out in great detail in this chapter.

I think most practicing Catholics, and small-town priests, are Christ-loving Christians like myself. They are simply ignorant to what the Holy See and Vatican are really all about. They've been deceived to take part in practices that are pagan in nature, and are associated with *Babylonian* gods of old. These fellow Christians don't know any better. They were just raised that way. Hopefully, after reading this compelling chapter, they will know better.

Starting with the first two verses, we find this woman called "great whore that sitteth upon many waters." The word "whore," more often than not in the Bible, alludes to spiritual fornication. There are a few verses that speak of literal whores or harlots, but it most always describes the people of God committing adultery against their Creator. All throughout God's Word, whenever Jews or Israel were unfaithful to YHWH, He'd say that they committed "whoredom" and they were called "harlots." The Church (global body of Christians) is described as the Bride of Christ. Therefore, when believers or entire denominations turn their backs on Jesus, entertaining false gods or pagan practices, they are unfaithful and committing spiritual whoredom.

The word "waters" in the Bible is often used symbolically to describe nations. The words "sitteth upon" imply that she is like a ruler sitting upon a throne ruling over many nations, but she will not be a political leader. She will be a religious ruler, though the power she wields is more similar to political rule than religious. The Catholic Church has long been the most dominant religious group in the world. It has a presence in virtually every nation on the planet. It is the largest denomination in Christianity, claiming about 1.3-billion members.

She also commits fornication with "the kings of the earth." Again, this is not describing physical relations but rather spiritual adultery. The woman will be in bed with the secular rulers of this world, and will sin against our God through her relationships with them. She will compromise on Biblical laws, morals, values, and doctrines of the Faith, in exchange for power, riches, and political influence. Throughout history, Popes have crowned or dethroned kings and the leaders of nations. The Church of Rome is the only Christian denomination that receives visits from ambassadors of nations and even Presidents. The Pope is viewed by many as the most powerful man and ruler on the earth.

In verse 3, John says that she'll sit upon the beast (the global kingdom of Antichrist). In previous chapters, I have written about the False Prophet possibly being the Pope. I said he could bring all religions of the world together into one global body to worship the Antichrist as god. So, it makes sense that the Church of Rome would be closely allied with the Beast, and also be the dominant religion of his world system.

Next, we read the beast will be "full of names of blasphemy." I believe this alludes not only to Antichrist being called by names and titles that are exclusive to God and Jesus, but also to names of false gods that will be incorporated into the One-World-Religion. For instance, Allah (Baal), Buddha, Shiva, and many other pagan gods of the world. We are then told that the beast will have "seven heads and ten horns." The angel reveals later in the Chapter that seven heads are "seven mountains, on which the woman sitteth." We also learn the ten horns will be "ten kings" who receive power during the Antichrist's global reign.

The ten kings, quite possibly Islamic (Daniel 11:39), hate and destroy the Roman Church - specifically Vatican City. They will topple and burn all its ancient structures and statues that bear any semblance to the Christian Faith. During the second half of the Tribulation, Christianity and Judaism will both be *public enemy number one* in the Antichrist's world order. I suspect the absolute desolation of Vatican City, which could serve as headquarters for the One-World-Religion, will be what causes the False Prophet's religion to be transferred from the *Mystery* Babylon in Rome unto the *literal* Babylon in the Mideast. I suggest you read Zechariah 5:7-11, which says that *the woman* is carried to Shinar (Babylon).

In verse 4 of Revelation 17, John describes the woman being "arrayed in purple and scarlet colour, and decked with gold and precious stones and pearls." The *Catholic Encyclopedia* says that the color of a "Cappa Magna" cloak, worn by bishops, is made of *purple* wool. When worn by cardinals, it is *scarlet* watered silk. The "Cassock" or "Soutane" robe (the official garb of the Roman Catholic clergy) is *purple* in color for bishops and other prelates and *scarlet* for cardinals. This is a very convincing reason for the Church of Rome being Mystery Babylon. While there are some Prophecy teachers who say she is Islam, USA, or even Jerusalem, none of these have specific connections to the colors worn by the woman. Only Catholicism does.

As for her being "decked with gold and precious stones and pearls," look at the garb worn by the Pope and instruments used in church services. They are decorated with gold, jewels, precious stones, and pearls. The Roman Church is by far one of the richest institutions in the entire world - and it's "a church," mind you, so that raises a red flag for me.

John goes on to say she has a "golden cup in her hand full of abominations and filthiness of her fornication." Could this refer to the golden chalice held up during every Communion ceremony of Catholic Mass? Possibly. But I'm not too dogmatic about it. What we need to pay attention to is not so much the cup itself, but what John says is inside it - "ABOMINATIONS and filthiness." These two things go hand in hand with the title of the woman that is given in the next verse:

Mystery, Babylon The Great, The Mother Of Harlots And Abominations Of The Earth

There is so much information to unpack concerning her title. First, "Mystery" obviously means that she is *not* literal Babylon. She'll be similar to the Babylon of old, but will also be something quite different altogether. Growing up as a Roman Catholic, I can tell you that the word *mystery* was sure used an awful lot in the Church. The Catholic Catechism refers to sacraments and liturgy

112

as "mysteries." Coincidence or connection? "The Great" denotes that she'll be the most dominant and powerful religious influence in the world to have roots in actual Babylon. I'll explain why the Catholic Church does in a moment. She is called "The Mother of Harlots And Abominations." This means she engages in hardcore idolatry, which the Holy Bible calls spiritual harlotry. She'll also be associated with literal harlots, believe it or not. I'll touch more on that as we go further. Her "abominations" refer to her many sins against the God of gods; whether idolatry, lies and deceptions, heresy, blasphemy, anti-Semitism, murder, greed, lust, Christian persecution, or countless other violations of God's Law. I am sure some of you are saying, "Christian persecution? This woman can't possibly be the Catholic Church then!" I once thought the same until I studied the history of the Roman Church. You will be just as shocked as I was when I reveal what I have discovered in my research.

First, let me address the idolatry or "harlotry" of the Roman Church. The reason that I keep referring to the Catholic Church as the "Roman Church" is because I believe that the institution is much more a product of Roman emperors, like Constantine, than it is of Christ's disciples and apostles - such as Peter or Paul. I say this because the Roman Catholic Church has historically meshed ancient pagan practices together with Christian ones. Even today, Catholic Churches in foreign nations mix Christianity with New Age beliefs, Hinduism, Buddhism, and even Voodoo. This is not surprising, because Constantine made it acceptable for the Roman Church to mingle paganism with Christianity.

After two centuries of Roman persecution of the Christians, Constantine had ended the war on believers in order to gain their approval and submission. He most certainly did. He is revered as a saint by Catholic and Orthodox Churches, though his supposed conversion to Christianity is a matter of debate among historians. The widely held view is that, even if he did convert, he held on to pagan influences and blended them with his Christianity. Proof of this can be found in the Catholic Church's symbols that pertain to worship of Rome's "Sun god" - which stemmed from *Babylon*.

For instance, the obelisk was a pillar erected by ancient pagan cultures as a monument to worship the Sun god. Atop the obelisk was a pyramid. The pyramid was the symbol for the Sun god of Egypt, known as "Ra." If you visit some of the largest Catholic churches in the world today, you'll be surprised to find an obelisk somewhere on church property. There is *no Biblical connection* to obelisks. Yet, these tall pillars stand in front of Catholic churches with an Egyptian pyramid atop them. Some of these obelisks may contain a Cross at the top, in order to make them appear Christian in nature, but in between the pyramid and a Cross you'll find the SUN - the most prominent symbol of ancient Sun god worship.

There is an obelisk in Rome's Vatican square in front of St. Peter's Basilica, and in front of the Pantheon in Rome. If you ever visit the Vatican, observe your surroundings closely. You will find dozens, if not hundreds, of images and symbols of the Sun in and around some of the most prominent sites in Catholicism. On top of this, the Monstrance (vessel used to display Eucharistic bread) is in the form of *the Sun*. But the Sun is not the only symbol of idolatry that you will find in a Roman Catholic Church. Whether dragons, serpents, beasts, or statues of men, idols are everywhere. The interior architecture of the Paul VI Audience Hall resembles the head of a serpent, and the Pope's seat is positioned inside its mouth. We all know who "the serpent" represents in the Bible.

You'd think the largest Christian denomination in this world would know the Ten Commandments, but the Catholic Church of Rome seems to be oblivious to the Second Commandment: "You shall not make for yourself an image in the form of anything in heaven above or on the earth beneath or in the waters below. You shall not bow down to them or worship them" (Exodus 20:4-5). I was surprised to find that the Vatican is not ignorant of the 2nd

Commandment at all. No, they know it all too well. So much so, they actually OMIT it from their list of the Commandments! They blatantly *removed* a Commandment of God. Have they never read Deuteronomy 4:2 and 12:32? Revelation 22:18? Yet, they expect Catholics to trust *them* to "interpret" the Bible?!

The Catholic Church states that images and statues should be "venerated by the faithful." Yet, God says the opposite! *Honoring* saints like Mary, Peter, Paul, and holy angels like Michael, is not idolatrous in itself; but when you bow down to or *worship* brass, wood, or stone, statues of them, that is the textbook definition of idolatry. Throughout the Bible, whenever a man of God tried to bow down and worship an angel of the LORD, he was rebuked by the angel (Revelation 19:10 and 22:8-9). There is nothing wrong with having images or statues of Lord Jesus, his holy Mother, or angels, in your home or church. It does become wrong when you begin to worship them.

I have countless images of Christ in my home. Too many to count actually. They show all visitors to my home Whom I love and serve. I like to surround myself with what I love. The only Holy Figure that we are commanded to never make an image or likeness of is YHWH, our God and Father in Heaven. While Jesus is the representation of God on the earth, His images depict Him in earthly form. We have not yet witnessed what He looks like in His glorified state, and nor has anyone ever seen YaHWeH in His Glory (John 1:18). Yet, the Roman Church (the denomination that refers to themselves as the "true Church") has images in churches depicting our Father in Heaven as an old man. That is a sin. You can *never* create an image of YHWH for any reason.

Besides their idolatry, Rome could be known as "Mother of Harlots" for another reason - for being a *literal* mother of harlots! Pope Pius II had once said, "Rome has more prostitutes than any other city because she has the most celibates." This unBiblical burden of celibacy, forced upon Catholic clergy, has caused many so-called men of God to commit the most depraved acts of sexual sins. Some Popes have fathered illegitimate children through sex with prostitutes, and you should be familiar with the large number of "celibate" priests that've been exposed for sexually molesting children. Also, homosexual priests are dying of aids worldwide. It has been estimated that around 70% of priests in some seminaries are *practicing* homosexuals.

Another abomination of the Roman Church is anti-Semitism. Since its inception, the Catholic Church has peddled the demonic lie that "the Jews killed Jesus." If that is the case, then how can they claim a Jew as being the sole reason for their existence? The Church claims that Peter, Jesus' *Jewish* disciple, was the very first Pope. Also, Lord Jesus *was a Jew* - along with 99% of his earliest followers. All the books of our Bible, with the exception of only two, were written by *Jews*. How can you hate the authors of the Book that you claim to represent and live by?

Because of the Roman Church's animosity toward Jews, they actually wholeheartedly supported Hitler! That demonic madman murdered six-million Jews in the Holocaust. Catholic bishops in Germany told their congregations that "the Church must mobilize all spiritual and moral forces in order to strengthen the Fuehrer." During the Holocaust, a Rabbi sent a letter to the Vatican begging the Pope to help the Jews who were being murdered by Hitler's Nazi Regime - especially the children. The reply of the Papacy was nothing short of Satanic. A representative for Pope Pius XII had replied to the Rabbi, "There is no such thing as the innocent blood of Jewish children! All Jewish blood is guilty, and the Jews must die because that is their punishment for that sin."

Archbishop Aloysius Stepinac is quoted as saying, "God has given us Adolf Hitler." Stepinac is now an official "saint" of the Catholic Church. During Hitler's reign of terror, Nazi Swastikas were even placed on Catholic altars. Adolf Hitler, because of the support he received from the Church, remained a Catholic until the end. The leadership and clergy of the Church didn't stand up to Hitler, and even supported him, because they had long held the anti-Semitic view of "Replacement Theology."

This unBiblical doctrine purports that God is "done" with the Nation of Israel and Jewish people, and that the Catholic Church has become the "new Israel" of God. Thus, they believe that they are now inheritors of every promise and blessing that the LORD ever pronounced upon Israel. The Church also teaches that Rome has become the "new" Jerusalem. Again... unBiblical. Catholics also use the titles that God specifically used to describe Jerusalem for Rome: the Holy City, the City of God, and the Eternal City.

Since Israel's reestablishment on the world scene in 1948, it took Roman Catholic leadership 46 years to simply acknowledge the existence of the Jewish State. The Church also abolished the Biblical Sabbath (Saturday), and replaced it with Sunday, because of its connection to the Jews and Israel. If Catholics would read their Bibles for themselves, they'd see that no such changes were ever made by God. I also encourage Catholic brothers and sisters to read Romans, Chapter 11, and see that your Church is poking God in the Eye with high-minded claims against Israel. Not wise!

You cannot read the Bible, cover to cover, and not recognize that without Israel we wouldn't have a Bible! The whole Book - Old and New Testaments - is *their* story. It is a love story not just between God and man, but specifically between YHWH and His chosen Nation of Israel. The Jewish State has always been called the Holy Land for a reason. It is where 99% of the events in the Bible occurred. There is no question that Israel is the holiest place on God's green earth. It always has been and it always will be - not Rome, and not anywhere else on Earth!

On top of their hostility toward the Jewish people and Israel, the Catholic Church says that "Muslims serve the same Creator" and are included in His plan of salvation. Sure, they can be saved if they come to Jesus, but are *not saved* now! It's blasphemous for any Church to say they are, and worse blasphemy to claim Allah of Islam is the same as YHWH of Judaism and Christianity. I had written extensively about why these two Gods are not the same in *The Signs of Our Times.* Read chapter 3 of that book for the proof from both the Holy Bible and the Quran.

I have previously stated that I believe the Pope could be the False Prophet. If not Pope Francis, then one like him in the future. It just makes the most Biblical sense. Since the Church is friendly with Islam, while also anti-Israel, it just bolsters my argument for the One-World-Religion being headquartered in Vatican City.

Another abomination of Catholicism is the deception and lies taught by the Vatican. The biggest lie they tell is that "the Church is *necessary for salvation* (Vatican II)." They say if you refuse to become Catholic, or leave their Church for another denomination of Christianity, then you cannot be saved. This is a blasphemous and unBiblical lie from the pit of Hell! All men and women of the earth are saved through Christ Jesus *alone* - not by any Church or body of men, not by good deeds, not by prayer, not by tithing, nor by religious practices, but by only one Name: JESUS.

The Roman Church has always demanded total subservience from their flock, and so they scare the faithful into submission by saying that they'll be damned if they don't follow everything that the "Holy Church" says. This isn't the way that Christ wants any church (body of believers) to be run. If you are Catholic, please don't believe the lie that you will lose your salvation if you don't follow everything your Church teaches. The Bible is clear when it states that there are only *two* simple things we must do to be truly saved, and they are:

"CONFESS WITH YOUR MOUTH THE LORD JESUS AND BELIEVE IN YOUR HEART THAT GOD HAS RAISED HIM FROM THE DEAD, AND YOU WILL BE SAVED. FOR WITH YOUR HEART YOU BELIEVE AND ARE JUSTIFIED, AND WITH YOUR MOUTH YOU CONFESS AND ARE SAVED." - ROMANS 10:9-10 AND ACTS 16:31

Not once in the Word of God has it ever been written that you must believe in "a Church," or teachings of Councils, or some guy with a pointy hat named "Pope," in order to be saved. Not once! All we are commanded to do is *confess* and *believe*, and then we are *saved*. God has made it simple, because He wills for all to be saved. So, keep it simple!

Besides saying that you need to believe in *them* in order to be saved, the Roman Church also teaches one *must* perform works, engage in Church rituals, and receive Church sacraments, in order to *be sure* of salvation. If you don't perform enough of these in your lifetime, then they say you'll have to suffer in purgatory until *you earn* your salvation. Wrong again! I think I've made it crystal clear that salvation requires JESUS CHRIST PLUS NOTHING. His sinless shed Blood on the Cross for the sins of mankind saves us. That is it! End of story. These false teachings of the Vatican explain why Catholics are taught to leave "interpretation" of the Holy Bible to their clergy alone.

In the early centuries of the Church, especially throughout the dark ages, Christians weren't even allowed to possess Bibles. The Holy Book was confiscated by the Church of Rome when it was found in the average citizen's possession. All those found with it were imprisoned, tortured, or murdered (at the hands of Catholic clergy). What kind of Church of God murders fellow believers for owning the Word of God that they supposedly represent? This is a huge reason why the Catholic Church could be Mystery Babylon.

Another lie of the Vatican that leads many Biblically-illiterate Catholics astray is that the Pope (and anything that he teaches) is "infallible," and that he is the *final word* on all matters. Catholics are to treat his word as Biblical "doctrine." Believe it or not, the Vatican actually teaches that when God's Word and words of the Pope are at odds, the opinion of the Pope *trumps* the Bible! This is heresy to the highest degree. Yet, if a Catholic challenges this dogma, then it's *they* who are dubbed a heretic. The Biblical truth is that no man or woman on Planet Earth has ever been infallible except for one Man, the *God-Man*, Jesus Christ. The Pope is not perfect. None of us are. We all need a Saviour - Pope included!

I ask Catholics believing the Pope's word trumps all, and that he's infallible, to study the history of the Papacy. You will see the fallacy of the infallibility claim. Here are a few examples -

❖ Pope Sergius III obtained the Papal office by murder.

❖ Pope John XII committed blasphemy, incest, adultery, simony, and murder.

❖ Pope Innocent III instituted the Inquisition which killed over one-million people (mostly Christians and Jews).

❖ Pope Sixtus IV sold offices and positions in the Church, and made his nephews cardinals.

❖ Pope Benedict IX committed adultery and murder.

❖ Pope Boniface VIII, believe it or not, was an atheist! That explains why he was a heretic and committed simony.

❖ Pope Alexander VI committed incest with his sister *and* with his daughter.

Wow, there were some real holy and infallible leaders in the Roman Church throughout the centuries (sarcasm intended). One of the sins that I mentioned which you may not be familiar with is *simony*. The term gets its name from a New Testament character, Simon the sorcerer. In the Book of Acts, Chapter 8, we read that he abandoned his sorcery, and was baptized as a Christian, after seeing all the signs, wonders, and miracles, being wrought by the disciples and apostles in the Name of Jesus. But he had become jealous of their powers, and offered them money in the hope that he could *buy* the gift of the Spirit. He was quickly and harshly rebuked by Peter.

This is why the buying or selling of ecclesiastical offices and privileges, such as positions of power within a church, pardons, or benefits, is known as simony. The Holy Spirit, the Kingdom of God, and salvation are not for sale. They are all given freely by YHWH unto all who believe in His Son, Jesus, as Lord. Still, so many Popes throughout history sold indulgences (forgiveness of sins granted by the Pope) or "tickets to Heaven" (meaning, for the right price, you could buy your way into Heaven). Both of these practices are 100% antithetical to what the Bible actually teaches.

#1: Only God can forgive sins, and He has made crystal clear over 1,000 times in His Word that there's just ONE way to obtain His forgiveness; and it is not through prayer, nor performing good deeds, or receiving communion, attending church, being baptized, and especially not through "indulgences." It is only through belief in the sacrifice of His only begotten Son on the Cross. Our sins are only washed away in the Blood of Jesus. Nothing and no one else will ever bring us God's forgiveness and salvation.

#2: You can never buy your salvation or a place in Heaven. The only way you can ever get there is to repent of your sins, and believe in the sinless life, death, resurrection, ascension, and the imminent return of Jesus Christ. He alone guarantees you a spot in Heaven. Again, absolutely nothing and no one else could ever promise you eternal life. Read JOHN 3:16. Whosoever believeth!

In verse 6 of Chapter 17, we read that she's "drunken with the blood of the saints, and the blood of the martyrs of Jesus." This is John's way of saying the blood of countless Jews and Christians was shed at her hands, and being *drunk* means she shed an awful lot of it. The Church of Rome burned hundreds of thousands of professing Christians at the stake for refusing to participate in the

121

rituals of Catholic Mass. Since at least 1183 AD, and for about five centuries, the view of the Roman Church was that "departure from their teaching was punishable by death." In the Inquisition, Bible-believing CHRISTIANS were put to death for refusing to pledge allegiance to Popes. Even women and children had been slaughtered... by a so-called "church." Disgusting.

I was shocked to discover that the Catholic Church martyred more Christians than pagan Rome or Islam ever have! This would explain John's statement about the woman at the close of verse 6 - "When I saw her, I wondered with great admiration." This is a poor translation of the Greek. The word for "admiration" means "astonished." This would imply that John was surprised, shocked, and startled by what he had seen. The group representing Mystery Babylon that John saw persecuting the Christians wasn't someone he'd expected. If the woman is representing Islam (as some Bible Prophecy teachers suggest), or some other religion of the world, I don't think that John would have been shocked at all.

The fact he'd been taken aback by what the angel had shown him signifies he saw people associated with the Cross of Christ murdering fellow Christians. I can think of no other reason why he would be astonished at the sight of Christian persecution. He'd already been shown visions of believers being martyred. Next, in verse 7, we read that she is carried by "the beast"; and this beast represents the kingdom of Antichrist. It will have seven heads and ten horns. The angel explains to John that these seven heads are seven mountains on which she sitteth. The Catholic Encyclopedia says "It is within the city of Rome, called *the city of seven hills*, that the entire area of Vatican proper is confined." So, the Roman Church is literally headquartered in a *city of seven mountains*.

In verse 10, John's told about the seven kings. The angel says that "five are fallen, and one is, and the other is not yet come; and when he cometh, he must continue a short space." The angel goes on to say that an "eighth" king will arise out "of the seven" (verse

11). This is all very confusing to the average reader, and so I will break it down for you. In order to have a king, you must have a kingdom. We know that Satan has controlled six kingdoms of the world throughout history, and that he'll revive the 6th in the Last Days. This gives us *seven* kingdoms - Egypt, Assyria, Babylon, Persia, Greece, Rome, and a revived Rome. The final kingdom is known as "the beast," and will be ruled by the eighth king who will rise out of the seven - the Antichrist.

I believe that his kingdom (of the seven) will be Assyrian or Babylonian in nature. An Old Testament title of Antichrist is "the *Assyrian*," and many End Times scholars believe he will set up his kingdom's headquarters in literal *Babylon* (as do I). The "ten horns" are described in verse 12 as ten kings who come to power during Antichrist's reign. They will be totally subservient to him and his kingdom. Earlier, I'd explained why they would hate the woman and eventually destroy her. In verse 14, they will attempt to make war on Jesus Himself! Of course, they will fail miserably (which is the greatest understatement of all time). I'll address this verse more in the coming chapter.

The number one reason why I believe Mystery Babylon could be the Catholic Church is what John reveals in verse 18 - "And the woman which thou sawest is that *great city*, which reigneth over the kings of the earth." When John wrote Revelation, what was the "great city" reigning over the whole earth at that time? The answer is ROME.

Chapter 18 of Revelation describes the destruction of what I believe to be the city of Rome, or Vatican City. Upon reading the Chapter, after digesting all that I have written, it is hard to argue otherwise. In verse 7, we read that she "glorified herself, and lived deliciously." Sound like Vatican City to you? It sure does to me. The latter half of this verse says that "she saith in her heart, I sit a queen, and am no widow." The Roman Church refers to Mary as the "Queen of Heaven," though the Bible never calls her this. God called Israel a "widow" whenever they turned their backs on Him. Today, the Church of Rome claims to be the "new" Israel and that Vatican City is the "new" Jerusalem. This is not Biblical, and rubs salt in Israel's wounds.

More proof for Revelation's Babylon being Rome is found in verses 22-23: "the voice of harpers, and musicians, and of pipers, and trumpeters, shall be heard no more at all in thee... And the light of a candle shall shine no more at all in thee; and the voice of the bridegroom and of the bride shall be heard no more at all in thee." All of these things are found within the Catholic Church. I think that "the voice of the *bridegroom*" is a spiritual reference to Lord Jesus Christ, meaning that the Popes, bishops, cardinals, and top brass of the Church, will no longer hear His voice through the Holy Spirit of God.

If this chapter has not convinced you that Mystery Babylon could be associated with the Roman Catholic Church, then I refer you to a book by Dave Hunt: *A Woman Rides the Beast*. The book is filled with over 500 pages on this subject, and goes into much greater detail than I could in one chapter of a book. I recommend it to anyone seeking a better understanding of the Roman Church.

Rome is no doubt set for a big fall in the near future. Another city that is set for a big fall, is one that does not even exist as I am writing this - *literal* Babylon. It does not exist because it has been uninhabited for centuries. During that time, there have been a few people who have passed through, toured, or excavated it. Saddam Hussein, the former Iraqi President, attempted to rebuild it for his Capital. He managed to build his palace there, but could not finish rebuilding the rest of the ancient city. There are many who believe that the city hasn't been rebuilt because it is fulfilling the ancient prophecy of Babylon's destruction in Isaiah 13; but I do not think that the Isaiah prophecy has been fulfilled.

If you read prophecies of Babylon in Isaiah, Chapters 13-14, and in Jeremiah, Chapters 50-51, it is hard to argue that they have come to pass. Here are five reasons why they have not:

❖ Babylon's destruction is to take place during the *"Day of the Lord"* (Great Tribulation).

❖ When Persia captured Babylon, they did so without a battle. That does not fit Isaiah's prophecy.

❖ Babylon will be destroyed "as Sodom and Gomorrah" were. That has never happened.

❖ Babylon will be uninhabited forever after its destruction. People have inhabited it since its fall.

❖ Israel is *in their own land* when Babylon is destroyed. Jews were not back in their Homeland when Babylon was captured centuries ago. Israel was not reborn until 1948.

If the prophecies of Isaiah and Jeremiah haven't been fulfilled to the letter, then they have not been fulfilled! No prophecy of the LORD has ever failed. So, rest assured that the Babylon prophecy will not be the first. The destruction of Babylon is coming, but not until Antichrist sets up the seat of his kingdom there. Indeed, Babylon *will* rise again... and will FALL.

BABYLON THE GREAT IS FALLEN, IS FALLEN, AND IS BECOME THE HABITATION OF DEVILS, AND THE HOLD OF EVERY FOUL SPIRIT, AND A CAGE OF EVERY UNCLEAN AND HATEFUL BIRD.

- REVELATION 18:2

CHAPTER TWELVE

ARMAGEDDON AND CHRIST'S RETURN

AND HE GATHERED THEM TOGETHER INTO A PLACE CALLED
IN THE HEBREW TONGUE ARMAGEDDON.

- REVELATION 16:16

ARMAGEDDON IS THE ONE word synonymous with the End
Times that is known to believers and unbelievers alike. What took
me by surprise, in my research, is there's far more to the Battle of
Armageddon than I originally thought. I always assumed that the
nations would gather in Megiddo when they come against Israel,
and ultimately against Almighty God. Then, they'd be destroyed
by our Lord in that place. It turns out that the war to end all wars
is fought in multiple locations! This came as a big surprise to me.
Sites of the battle between Antichrist's armies and armies of our
Lord are Babylon, Jerusalem, Bozrah in Jordan, and Megiddo.

I have come to discover that the least amount of confrontation
between Jesus and the Antichrist will take place in Megiddo, and
it serves as more of a staging area for the coalition of nations that
take up arms alongside Antichrist. *Armageddon* stems from "Har
Megiddo" (Hebrew), and means Mount Megiddo. It is a relatively
small mountainous area in the Jezreel Valley, southeast of Haifa.

Taking a look back at Chapter 16, where Armageddon is first
mentioned, we find that demonic spirits are sent forth from the

mouths of the Satanic trinity - the dragon (Satan), the Antichrist (son of Satan), and the False Prophet (religious leader) - unto the kings "of the whole world." These spirits will influence the world leaders to gather together at Megiddo for "the battle of that great day of God Almighty." What message could have been sent to the kings that would lead them all to come against the Jewish State?

I believe the Two Witnesses being resurrected, and taken into Heaven in the sight of the whole world, will be a major blow to the kingdom of Antichrist. We read in Chapter 11 that the Jews of Jerusalem who survived the great earthquake, which followed the ascension of the Witnesses, gave glory to YHWH. This will cause Jews to finally see Antichrist for what he truly is: a false messiah representing Satan. As they preach this truth unto fellow Jews of Israel, who'd easily believe after witnessing the Beast commit the abomination of desolation inside their Temple's Holy of Holies, the Beast will set out to destroy them. Thus, the message that will be sent out to the nations of the world will be an anti-Semitic one.

It will sound reminiscent of a speech by Hitler. Through the demonic spirits, the devil will speak the lie that the Jewish people are the reason for all catastrophes that befell Earth throughout the course of the past seven years. Antichrist might say it is because they continue to worship "the false god" (referring to YHWH and Lord Jesus Christ) why the world's been plagued with the sores, darkness, great earthquakes, cosmic chaos, and historic disasters. To restore peace, calm, and normalcy to Planet Earth, he will say that the Jews and their Nation must be dealt with swiftly; and the kings of Earth will buy into his lies. Once the nations are gathered in Megiddo, Antichrist and his armies will meet them there.

Now, remember when I said that I thought the literal Babylon of the Mideast will be the headquarters of the Antichrist, and that it would fall in the near future? It is at this time that I foresee this prophecy being fulfilled. Due to the Beast taking all his firepower and military defenses out of his home base to make war on Jews in Israel, it will leave the door wide open for his enemies to come and destroy Babylon as Isaiah and Jeremiah prophesied long-ago. The prophecies of Babylon's destruction "in the Day of the Lord" are found in Isaiah - Chapters 13 and 14, and Jeremiah - Chapters 50 and 51. These prophecies align with another about Antichrist in Daniel - Chapter 11:40-45.

I recommend that you read all of these Chapters and verses in one sitting, with Chapters 16 and 19 of Revelation, in order to see the complete picture of what God has planned for the Beast and his kingdom in the end. The aforementioned prophecies of Isaiah and Jeremiah say Jews in Israel will rejoice over the destruction of the global seat of the Antichrist. If the Beast didn't loathe them before, he will have nothing but bloodthirsty murderous thoughts toward them now. This leads to the next phase of Armageddon. In his anger, Antichrist leads the armies of the world from Megiddo into the Holy City of Jerusalem to utterly destroy it.

When prophesying to His disciples about what would occur during the Great Tribulation, Lord Jesus said, "When ye shall see Jerusalem compassed with armies, then know that the desolation thereof is nigh, Then let them which are in Judaea *flee to the mountains*; and let them which are in the midst of it depart out; and let not them that are in the countries enter thereinto" (Luke 21:20-21, Matthew 24:16, and Mark 13:14). Through a thorough study of the Old Testament, I suspect that "the mountains" which the Jews flee to are in Jordan - specifically Bozrah (also known as Petra). It is a mountainous region filled with caves where they can hide themselves from the armies of Antichrist.

Israelis who do not heed that command of our Lord, to flee Jerusalem, will fall victim to Antichrist's violent siege of the City. Zechariah 14:2 says "the city shall be taken, houses rifled, and the women ravished; and half of the city shall go forth into captivity." During his campaign against Jerusalem, Antichrist sends some of his army to destroy the remnant of the Jews that fled to Bozrah.

When he is finished with the Holy City, he too will head to Jordan to finish off the Jews that fled; but, to his dismay, he is going to find that Someone else had already beat him there.

Yes, just when Satan thinks he is finally victorious over God's people, after destroying much of their God-given Holy Land, the second greatest event in history occurs - the Second Coming of Jesus Christ! Obviously, the *greatest* event was His First Coming. I believe that the Jews, after coming under attack by the Beast and his armies, will finally call out to Jesus as their Messiah and Lord (Psalms 79 & 80, Joel 2:32 and Matthew 23:39). Isaiah paints the picture that will have the Antichrist shaking in his boots -

"WHO IS THIS THAT COMETH FROM EDOM, WITH DYED GARMENTS FROM BOZRAH? THIS THAT IS GLORIOUS IN HIS APPAREL, TRAVELLING IN THE GREATNESS OF HIS STRENGTH? I THAT SPEAK IN RIGHTEOUSNESS, MIGHTY TO SAVE." - ISAIAH 63:1

Antichrist and his armies witness Christ coming from Bozrah, with the Jews that fled there, the saints of Heaven, and His angels, in tow. The armies of Heaven finally come down to put an end to Satan's Godless armies of the world once and for all. Our Lord officially made His return before He rescued the Jews in Bozrah, when His feet touched down on the Mount of Olives -

"THE LORD SHALL GO FORTH, AND FIGHT AGAINST THOSE NATIONS, AS WHEN HE FOUGHT IN THE DAY OF BATTLE. AND HIS FEET SHALL STAND IN THAT DAY UPON THE MOUNT OF OLIVES, WHICH IS BEFORE JERUSALEM ON THE EAST, AND THE MOUNT OF OLIVES SHALL CLEAVE IN THE MIDST THEREOF TOWARD THE EAST AND TOWARD THE WEST, AND THERE SHALL BE A VERY GREAT VALLEY; AND HALF OF THE MOUNTAIN SHALL REMOVE TOWARD THE NORTH, AND HALF OF IT TOWARD THE SOUTH." - ZECHARIAH 14:3-4

"AND I SAW HEAVEN OPENED, AND BEHOLD A WHITE HORSE; AND HE THAT SAT UPON HIM WAS CALLED FAITHFUL AND TRUE, IN RIGHTEOUSNESS HE DOTH JUDGE AND MAKE WAR. HIS EYES WERE AS A FLAME OF FIRE, AND ON HIS HEAD WERE MANY CROWNS; AND HE HAD A NAME WRITTEN, THAT NO MAN KNEW, BUT HE HIMSELF. AND HE WAS CLOTHED WITH A VESTURE DIPPED IN BLOOD: AND HIS NAME IS CALLED THE WORD OF GOD. AND THE ARMIES WHICH WERE IN HEAVEN FOLLOWED HIM UPON WHITE HORSES, CLOTHED IN FINE LINEN, WHITE AND CLEAN. AND OUT OF HIS MOUTH GOETH A SHARP SWORD, THAT WITH IT HE SHOULD SMITE THE NATIONS: AND SHALL RULE THEM WITH A ROD OF IRON: AND HE TREADETH THE WINEPRESS OF THE FIERCENESS AND WRATH OF ALMIGHTY GOD. HE HATH ON HIS VESTURE AND ON HIS THIGH A NAME WRITTEN, KING OF KINGS, AND LORD OF LORDS." - REVELATION 19:11-16

"BEHOLD, THE LORD COMETH WITH TEN THOUSANDS OF HIS SAINTS." - JUDE 1:14

"THE SON OF MAN SHALL COME IN THE GLORY OF HIS FATHER WITH HIS ANGELS." - MATTHEW 16:27

"AND IT SHALL COME TO PASS IN THAT DAY, THAT I WILL SEEK TO DESTROY ALL THE NATIONS THAT COME AGAINST JERUSALEM, SAITH THE LORD GOD." - ZECHARIAH 12:9

At this time, I suspect that Antichrist and the kings with him - being filled with great fear - will flee back to Israel. They'll then reassemble in the valley of Jehoshaphat, which is just outside of Jerusalem. This would fulfill the prophecy of Joel, Chapter 3 and verses 2 and 12 -

"I WILL ALSO GATHER ALL NATIONS, AND WILL BRING THEM DOWN INTO THE VALLEY OF JEHOSHAPHAT, AND WILL JUDGE

THEM THERE ON BEHALF OF MY PEOPLE AND ON BEHALF OF MY HERITAGE ISRAEL."

"LET THE HEATHEN BE WAKENED, AND COME UP TO THE VALLEY OF JEHOSHAPHAT: FOR THERE WILL I SIT TO JUDGE ALL THE HEATHEN ROUND ABOUT."

Realizing they've got nowhere to run from the Lord of lords, and instead of repenting, the world's armies join the Antichrist in fighting against God in the flesh and His armies of Heaven. If this sounds to you as stupid, idiotic, and like they have a death wish, you're not alone. Someone else feels the same and *He laughs* at them. He being the LORD -

"WHY DO THE HEATHEN RAGE, AND THE PEOPLE IMAGINE A VAIN THING? THE KINGS OF THE EARTH SET THEMSELVES, AND THE RULERS TAKE COUNSEL TOGETHER, AGAINST THE LORD, AND AGAINST HIS ANOINTED, SAYING, LET US BREAK THEIR BANDS ASUNDER, AND CAST AWAY THEIR CORDS FROM US. HE THAT SITTETH IN THE HEAVENS SHALL LAUGH: THE LORD SHALL HAVE THEM IN DERISION. THEN SHALL HE SPEAK UNTO THEM IN HIS WRATH, AND VEX THEM IN HIS SORE DISPLEASURE. YET HAVE I SET MY KING UPON MY HOLY HILL OF ZION. I WILL DECLARE THE DECREE: THE LORD HATH SAID UNTO ME, THOU ART MY SON; THIS DAY HAVE I BEGOTTEN THEE. ASK OF ME, AND I SHALL GIVE THEE THE HEATHEN FOR THINE INHERITANCE, AND THE UTTERMOST PARTS OF THE EARTH FOR THY POSSESSION. THOU SHALT BREAK THEM WITH A ROD OF IRON; THOU SHALT DASH THEM IN PIECES LIKE A POTTER'S VESSEL. BE WISE NOW THEREFORE, O YE KINGS: BE INSTRUCTED, YE JUDGES OF THE EARTH. SERVE THE LORD WITH FEAR, AND REJOICE WITH TREMBLING. KISS THE SON, LEST HE BE ANGRY, AND YE PERISH FROM THE WAY, WHEN HIS WRATH IS KINDLED BUT A LITTLE. BLESSED ARE ALL THEY THAT PUT THEIR TRUST IN HIM." - PSALM 2

When Jesus and His armies arrive in Jehoshaphat, Antichrist and his armies attempt to fight Him but are put down swiftly (and that is an understatement) - simply by the spoken word of Jesus. He does not need to lift a finger against them, nor will His army raise a sword. Here's what Scripture says about the shortest battle in world history -

"THESE SHALL MAKE WAR WITH THE LAMB, AND THE LAMB SHALL OVERCOME THEM: FOR HE IS LORD OF LORDS, AND KING OF KINGS: AND THEY THAT ARE WITH HIM ARE CALLED, AND CHOSEN, AND FAITHFUL." - REVELATION 17:14

"THE LORD SHALL CONSUME THAT WICKED ONE WITH THE SPIRIT OF HIS MOUTH, AND SHALL DESTROY HIM WITH THE BRIGHTNESS OF HIS COMING." - 2ND THESSALONIANS 2:8

"AND I SAW THE BEAST, AND THE KINGS OF THE EARTH, AND THEIR ARMIES, GATHERED TOGETHER TO MAKE WAR AGAINST HIM THAT SAT ON THE HORSE, AND AGAINST HIS ARMY. AND THE BEAST WAS TAKEN, AND WITH HIM THE FALSE PROPHET THAT WROUGHT MIRACLES BEFORE HIM, WITH WHICH HE DECEIVED THEM THAT HAD RECEIVED THE MARK OF THE BEAST, AND THEM THAT WORSHIPPED HIS IMAGE. THESE BOTH WERE CAST ALIVE INTO A LAKE OF FIRE BURNING WITH BRIMSTONE. AND THE REMNANT WERE SLAIN WITH THE SWORD OF HIM THAT SAT UPON THE HORSE, WHICH SWORD PROCEEDED OUT OF HIS MOUTH: AND ALL THE FOWLS WERE FILLED WITH THEIR FLESH." - REVELATION 19:19-21

I'm sure that Satan will be extremely disappointed when this day comes. He managed to gather virtually every nation and army of the world to do battle with God and His Heavenly armies, and there wasn't even a fight. Lord Jesus showed up, spoke the word, and it was game over. Jesus wins. Not only are the Antichrist and

False Prophet thrown alive into the abyss, but Revelation 20 tells of how Satan will be chained up and cast into the pit with them. The LORD must have a sense of humor though, because He allows the devil one last hoorah after 1,000 years of being bound. Lucifer will again assemble nations of the world to come against the saints of God and His Holy City, Jerusalem. Yet, he and his armies will be wiped out quicker than they were the first time. So, don't blink! God Almighty will send fire from Heaven to devour them. Satan is then cast back into the lake of fire where he will be "tormented day and night for ever and ever."

If you were left behind and have lived through these events, congratulations, you will now reign with our Lord for 1,000 years from Jerusalem. After the Millennium, when the final judgments of humanity have convened, we'll rule and reign with Him in the NEW Earth from a NEW Jerusalem forever. What a glorious time it will be! So, take heart, THERE IS A HAPPY ENDING.

AND THE LORD SHALL BE KING OVER ALL THE EARTH: IN THAT DAY SHALL THERE BE ONE LORD, AND HIS NAME ONE.

- ZECHARIAH 14:9

EPILOGUE

A NEW HEAVEN AND A NEW EARTH

AND I SAW A NEW HEAVEN AND A NEW EARTH: FOR THE FIRST
HEAVEN AND THE FIRST EARTH WERE PASSED AWAY; AND
THERE WAS NO MORE SEA. AND I JOHN SAW THE HOLY CITY,
NEW JERUSALEM, COMING DOWN FROM GOD OUT OF
HEAVEN, PREPARED AS A BRIDE ADORNED FOR HER HUSBAND.

- REVELATION 21:1-2

I LIKE THE DESCRIPTION of Christ's Millennial Kingdom by Hal Lindsey in his book, *There's a New World Coming*. He said, "The sky will be bluer, the grass will be greener, the flowers will smell sweeter, the air will be cleaner, and man will be happier than he ever dreamed possible!" I do not think that you could ever describe it any better than that.

Zechariah (in Chapter 14 of his prophetic Book) and Ezekiel (in Chapters 40-48 of his Book) both describe the future of Israel during the Millennium. They write about a new glorious Temple being built in Jerusalem, and all nations of the earth coming up every year to worship YHWH there. Zechariah says that nations who do not come to worship God during the Feast of Tabernacles will receive no rain. Ezekiel gives great details concerning the Land allotment of the 12 Tribes during the Millennium. So, those who say that God is "done with Israel" have obviously never read the prophetic Books of the Bible. They detail the future of Israel more than any other nation or people in the history of the world. The LORD will *never* be done with Israel. Not ever!

Following the Millennial reign of Christ on the earth with His saints (Old Testament saints, resurrected Church, the martyrs, and those who had become believers during the Tribulation Hour), the remainder of the dead (all unbelievers throughout history) will be raised and judged. They'll then be cast into the lake of fire, along with Death and Hell (Revelation 20:11-15). Following this final judgment of mankind, John says he "saw a *new* heaven and a *new* earth: the first heaven and first earth were passed away; and there was no more sea" (Revelation 21:1).

After about 7,000 years of humans defiling this earth through sin, and following the destruction of at least half of it during the Tribulation, the LORD is finally going to unveil a new and perfect Earth. The planet will be filled with the beauty of the Garden of Eden, and there'll be no more seas or deserts. It'll be like Heaven on Earth. It will be the long desired answer to the Lord's Prayer we Christians have prayed for thousands of years: "Thy Kingdom come, Thy will be done, ON EARTH as it is in Heaven." Isaiah was given visions of this new Earth thousands of years ago, and he described it in Chapters 11 and 65 of his Book -

"THE WOLF ALSO SHALL DWELL WITH THE LAMB, AND THE LEOPARD SHALL LIE DOWN WITH THE KID; AND THE CALF AND THE YOUNG LION AND THE FATLING TOGETHER; AND A LITTLE CHILD SHALL LEAD THEM. AND THE COW AND THE BEAR SHALL FEED; THEIR YOUNG ONES SHALL LIE DOWN TOGETHER: AND THE LION SHALL EAT STRAW LIKE THE OX. THE SUCKING CHILD SHALL PLAY ON THE HOLE OF THE ASP (VENOMOUS SERPENT), AND THE WEANED CHILD SHALL PUT HIS HAND ON THE COCKATRICE' (POISONOUS SERPENT OR SMALL DRAGON-LIKE CREATURE) DEN. THEY SHALL NOT HURT NOR DESTROY IN ALL MY HOLY MOUNTAIN: THE EARTH

SHALL BE FULL OF THE KNOWLEDGE OF THE LORD, AS THE WATERS COVER THE SEA." - 11:6-9

"THEY SHALL BUILD HOUSES, AND INHABIT THEM; AND THEY SHALL PLANT VINEYARDS, AND EAT THE FRUIT OF THEM. THEY SHALL NOT BUILD, AND ANOTHER INHABIT; THEY SHALL NOT PLANT, AND ANOTHER EAT: FOR AS THE DAYS OF A TREE ARE THE DAYS OF MY PEOPLE, AND MINE ELECT SHALL LONG ENJOY THE WORK OF THEIR HANDS. THEY SHALL NOT LABOUR IN VAIN, NOR BRING FORTH FOR TROUBLE; FOR THEY ARE THE SEED OF THE BLESSED OF THE LORD, AND THEIR OFFSPRING WITH THEM. AND IT SHALL COME TO PASS, THAT BEFORE THEY CALL, I WILL ANSWER; AND WHILE THEY ARE YET SPEAKING, I WILL HEAR. THE WOLF AND THE LAMB SHALL FEED TOGETHER, AND THE LION SHALL EAT STRAW LIKE THE BULLOCK: AND DUST SHALL BE THE SERPENT'S MEAT. THEY SHALL NOT HURT NOR DESTROY IN ALL MY HOLY MOUNTAIN, SAITH THE LORD." - 65:17-25

As for the new Heaven, I am not sure if that means simply a new Universe or if God's Holy Heaven will also be recreated or renovated. I guess we will have to wait and see. I do not think that any human being will know for sure in this life. All I know is that He will make "all things new" (Revelation 21:5). One of the new things that He reveals the most information about, in Chapters 21 and 22 of Revelation, is the new Jerusalem. God's Holy City gets recreated, and John witnesses it descend from Heaven toward the earth. The new Jerusalem will be a sight to behold, as we'll learn going forward. It will be 2-million square miles, dwarfing earthly Jerusalem (48 square miles).

It'll be in the new Holy City where the LORD Himself dwells amongst His people (Revelation 21:3-4). Next, John says that he heard a great voice out of heaven saying, "Behold, the tabernacle of God is with men, and he will dwell with them, and they shall be his people, and God himself shall be with them, and be their

God. And God shall wipe away all tears from their eyes; there shall be no more death, neither sorrow, nor crying, neither shall there be any more pain: for the former things are passed away." Praise the Lord for that day!

"AND THE ANGEL CARRIED ME AWAY IN THE SPIRIT TO A GREAT AND HIGH MOUNTAIN, AND SHEWED ME THAT GREAT CITY, THE HOLY JERUSALEM, DESCENDING OUT OF HEAVEN FROM GOD, HAVING THE GLORY OF GOD: AND HER LIGHT WAS LIKE UNTO A STONE MOST PRECIOUS, EVEN LIKE A JASPER STONE, CLEAR AS CRYSTAL; AND HAD A WALL GREAT AND HIGH, AND HAD TWELVE GATES, AND AT THE GATES TWELVE ANGELS, AND NAMES WRITTEN THEREON, WHICH ARE THE NAMES OF THE TWELVE TRIBES OF THE CHILDREN OF ISRAEL: ON THE EAST THREE GATES; ON THE NORTH THREE GATES; ON THE SOUTH THREE GATES; AND ON THE WEST THREE GATES. AND THE WALL OF THE CITY HAD TWELVE FOUNDATIONS, AND IN THEM THE NAMES OF THE TWELVE APOSTLES OF THE LAMB. AND HE THAT TALKED WITH ME HAD A GOLDEN REED TO MEASURE THE CITY, AND THE GATES THEREOF, AND THE WALL THEREOF. AND THE CITY LIETH FOURSQUARE, AND THE LENGTH IS AS LARGE AS THE BREADTH: AND HE MEASURED THE CITY WITH THE REED, TWELVE THOUSAND FURLONGS. THE LENGTH AND THE BREADTH AND THE HEIGHT OF IT ARE EQUAL. HE MEASURED THE WALL THEREOF, AN HUNDRED AND FORTY AND FOUR CUBITS, ACCORDING TO THE MEASURE OF A MAN, THAT IS, OF THE ANGEL. AND THE BUILDING OF THE WALL OF IT WAS OF JASPER: AND THE CITY WAS PURE GOLD, LIKE UNTO CLEAR GLASS." - REVELATION 21:10-18

Here we are told that both the 12 Tribes of Israel and the 12 Apostles are represented in this City. Since the Scripture clearly says *apostles,* and not *disciples*, theologians infer that the Apostle Paul is included in the twelve to replace Judas - and not Matthias, who was chosen by lot. John will now give us a glimpse into the breathtaking beauty of the new Jerusalem -

"AND THE FOUNDATIONS OF THE WALL OF THE CITY WERE GARNISHED WITH ALL MANNER OF PRECIOUS STONES. THE FIRST FOUNDATION WAS JASPER; THE SECOND, SAPPHIRE; THE THIRD, A CHALCEDONY; THE FOURTH, AN EMERALD; THE FIFTH, SARDONYX; THE SIXTH, SARDIUS; THE SEVENTH, CHRYSOLYTE; THE EIGHTH, BERYL; THE NINTH, A TOPAZ; THE TENTH, A CHRYSOPRASUS; THE ELEVENTH, A JACINTH; THE TWELFTH, AN AMETHYST." - REVELATION 21:19-20

Wow. Can you imagine passing by these walls everyday? I'd like to insert a colorful picture here to convey the beauty of the City, but there is really no painting or picture out there that could possibly do the new Jerusalem justice. It is going to be one of the LORD's greatest and most beautiful creations, and believers will dwell in it someday. HalleluYah! If you still want an idea of just how amazing the City will be, take a look at the Emerald City in the *Wizard of Oz*. While that is a green-colored city, the image of the yellow brick road leading up to that sparkling city is the best possible image I could think of that is anywhere near comparable. As for the twelve precious stones...

Jasper is clear or gold. Associated with the Tribe of Simeon.

Sapphire is blue. Associated with the Tribe of Reuben.

Chalcedony is green. Associated with the Tribe of Naphtali.

Emerald is bright green. Associated with the Tribe of Asher.

Sardonyx is red. Associated with the Tribe of Dan.

Sardius is fiery-red. Associated with the Tribe of Levi.

Chrysolyte is yellow/gold. Associated with the Tribe of Zebulun.

Beryl is emerald green. Associated with the Tribe of Judah.

Topaz is a yellow and green mixture. Associated with the Tribe of Issachar.

Chrysoprasus is green. Associated with the Tribe of Benjamin.

Jacinth is violet. Associated with the Tribe of Joseph.

Amethyst is purple. Associated with the Tribe of Gad.

There are some students of the Holy Bible who may disagree on the exact colors of these stones, or as to which Tribes they are associated with, but I derived my conclusions from comparing the findings of four well-known and trusted theologians. As for what else John has to say about the new Jerusalem...

"THE TWELVE GATES WERE TWELVE PEARLS: EVERY SEVERAL GATE WAS OF ONE PEARL: AND THE STREET OF THE CITY WAS PURE GOLD, AS IT WERE TRANSPARENT GLASS. AND I SAW NO TEMPLE THEREIN: FOR THE LORD GOD ALMIGHTY AND THE LAMB ARE THE TEMPLE OF IT. AND THE CITY HAD NO NEED OF THE SUN, NEITHER OF THE MOON, TO SHINE IN IT: FOR THE GLORY OF GOD DID LIGHTEN IT, AND THE LAMB IS THE LIGHT THEREOF. THE NATIONS OF THEM WHICH ARE SAVED SHALL WALK IN THE LIGHT OF IT: AND THE KINGS OF THE EARTH DO BRING THEIR GLORY AND HONOUR INTO IT. AND THE GATES OF IT SHALL NOT BE SHUT AT ALL BY DAY: FOR THERE SHALL BE NO NIGHT THERE. AND THEY SHALL BRING THE GLORY AND HONOUR OF THE NATIONS INTO IT." - REVELATION 21:21-26

Our simple minds can't fathom the unparalleled beauty of the glorious City. Gates of pearls, and a street of gold! It may sound like a fairytale or fantasy; but just as every other prophecy of the LORD has come to pass throughout history, it will be a reality for all believers someday. The best part of the new Jerusalem is that it will be illuminated 24-7, every day and night, every week, every month, every season, and every year, by the Lord Himself. He is the Light of the world, and in Him there is no darkness (John 8:12 & 1st John 1:5). Imagine no more night or dark clouds ever again for eternity. As if all of this was not amazing enough, John still had even more to say -

"AND HE SHEWED ME A PURE RIVER OF WATER OF LIFE, CLEAR AS CRYSTAL, PROCEEDING OUT OF THE THRONE OF GOD AND OF THE LAMB. IN THE MIDST OF THE STREET OF IT, AND ON EITHER SIDE OF THE RIVER, WAS THERE THE TREE OF LIFE, WHICH BARE TWELVE MANNER OF FRUITS, AND YIELDED HER FRUIT EVERY MONTH: AND THE LEAVES OF THE TREE WERE FOR THE HEALING OF THE NATIONS. AND THERE SHALL BE NO MORE CURSE: BUT THE THRONE OF GOD AND OF THE LAMB SHALL BE IN IT; AND HIS SERVANTS SHALL SERVE HIM: AND THEY SHALL SEE HIS FACE; AND HIS NAME SHALL BE IN THEIR FOREHEADS. THERE SHALL BE NO NIGHT THERE; AND THEY NEED NO CANDLE, NEITHER LIGHT OF THE SUN; FOR THE LORD GOD GIVETH THEM LIGHT: AND THEY SHALL REIGN FOR EVER AND EVER. HE SAID UNTO ME, THESE SAYINGS ARE FAITHFUL AND TRUE: AND THE LORD GOD OF THE HOLY PROPHETS SENT HIS ANGEL TO SHEW UNTO HIS SERVANTS THE THINGS WHICH MUST BE DONE IN HASTE." - REVELATION 22:1-6

I believe the river of life and the tree of life are both literal in nature, but the thing we need to take notice of is that the life we receive from both come from God. He is the source. The eternal life and perfect health that the LORD brings in the new Jerusalem will proceed from the throne in a river of water. That water will nourish the roots of the tree of life - of which there may be many on each side of the river. "The twelve manner of fruits" continues the theme of the City being connected to the Tribes and Apostles.

The best news of all is that both YHWH and Lord Jesus are going to make their new home in the new Jerusalem! Up until the end, they both dwell in what the Bible calls the "Third Heaven" (2nd Corinthians 12:2). If you remember the earlier verses that I shared in this chapter, it was said that Heaven and Earth passed away. So, that is most likely why our God and Lord will dwell in the City. But, wait, there's still more! Not only will we serve God, and be able to enter into His presence, but we'll finally get to "see His face"! Something that every servant of the LORD has longed to do from the very beginning.

Also, while everyone that took the Mark of the Beast in their foreheads was cast into the lake of fire for eternity, all believers bear God's Name in our foreheads *in Paradise* for eternity. Who would ever want to take the first mark? And who wouldn't desire receiving the last mark? I can't wait to have His Name etched into my body forever. If you were left behind during the Tribulation, and read this before the Mark of the Beast is instituted, don't take the mark given by men! Wait for the mark that is given by God.

I hope to meet readers of this book in new Jerusalem one day; and I pray you'll all testify that this book helped lead you into the waiting arms of our loving Saviour. Only YOU have the final say as to whether or not either of these things come to pass. Make the right choice, because **Jesus is coming soon**.

BEHOLD, I COME QUICKLY: BLESSED IS HE THAT KEEPETH THE SAYINGS OF THE PROPHECY OF THIS BOOK.

- REVELATION 22:7

ACKNOWLEDGMENTS

TO YAHWEH, LORD JESUS, and the Holy Spirit, thank You for guiding me on the right path daily. Thank You for every blessing, and for all that are yet to come. Thank You for Your holy angels that surround us every day, and especially Michael the Archangel - who inspires the boldness and courage inside of me to stand up against all that is evil in this world. I love You forever my God.

To Mom, thanks for all that you have ever done for me in this life. My writing career would not have been possible without your help, inspiration, and constant encouragement. I love you always.

To my boy Jacob, Dad, my Brother, and the rest of my family, I appreciate you all and I love you all so very much. I have been blessed by every one of you in so many ways. It is my prayer that the LORD blesses you all abundantly for the joy that each of you have brought me in this life.

To the Benham Brothers (Jason and David), Chris S., and my faithful readers, thank you so much for all that you have done and do for me. I would not be where I am today if it were not for your advice, help, and support. You are all appreciated and loved. May our Good Lord bless and keep you all until the End.

NOTES

Introduction: Left Behind?

1. MichaEL Sawdy, *Even More Signs of Our Times* (Plymouth, MI: Biblical Signs Publishing, 2019), 9-14.

Chapter One: 4 Horsemen of the Apocalypse

1. MichaEL Sawdy, *The Signs of Our Times* (Plymouth, MI: Biblical Signs Publishing, 2018), 53.
2. MichaEL Sawdy, *Even More Signs of Out Times* (Plymouth, MI: Biblical Signs Publishing, 2019), 61-67.

Chapter Two: Fifth and Sixth Seals

1. Chuck Missler, "Revelation Session 13 Ch 6 Opening The Seals," 2013, accessed September 2019, https://youtu.be/RRvo9rPvtS8

Chapter Three: 144,000 Jewish Evangelists Sealed

1. Hal Lindsey, *There's A New World Coming* (Ventura, CA: Vision House Publishers, 1973/Bantam Edition, 1975), 108.

Chapter Four: Seventh Seal and Four Trumpets

1. John Macarthur, *Because the Time is Near* (Chicago, IL: Moody Publishers, 2007), 155-156.
2. Hal Lindsey, *Apocalypse Code* (Palos Verdes, CA: Western Front Ltd., 1997).
3. Hal Lindsey, *Planet Earth: The Final Chapter* (Beverly Hills, CA: Western Front Ltd., 1998).

CHAPTER FIVE: FIFTH AND SIXTH TRUMPETS

1. MichaEL Sawdy, *The Signs of Our Times* (Plymouth, MI: Biblical Signs Publishing, 2018), 73-75.
2. MichaEL Sawdy, *Even More Signs of Our Times* (Plymouth, MI: Biblical Signs Publishing, 2019), 70-74.

CHAPTER SIX: THE ANTICHRIST

1. MichaEL Sawdy, *The Signs of Our Times* (Plymouth, MI: Biblical Signs Publishing, 2018), Chapters 4, 5, 6, and 8.
2. MichaEL Sawdy, *Even More Signs of Our Times* (Plymouth, MI: Biblical Signs Publishing, 2019), Chapter 7.
3. "Comparing the Biblical Antichrist and the Mahdi," accessed September 2019, https://www.answering-islam.org/Authors/JR/Future/ch05_comp aring_the_biblical_antichrist.htm

CHAPTER SEVEN: THE FALSE PROPHET

1. Gerard O' Connell, "Pope Francis to World's Religious Leaders: We Build the Future Together or There Will Be No Future," February 4, 2019, https://www.americamagazine.org/faith/2019/02/04/pope-francis-worlds-religious-leaders-we-build-future-together-or-there-will-b e-no
2. "Is Pope Francis the False Prophet?," accessed September 2019, https://thewildvoice.org/is-pope-francis-false-prophet/
3. MichaEL Sawdy, *Even More Signs of Our Times* (Plymouth, MI: Biblical Signs Publishing, 2019), 111-116.
4. CNN, "White Smoke Signals New Pope," March 13, 2019, accessed October 2019, https://youtu.be/rYvb5CiUt6s

CHAPTER EIGHT: MARK OF THE BEAST

1. Walid Shoebat, "Mark of the Beast," April 29, 2008, accessed October 2019, https://youtu.be/GtquNNEO7Fw

2. MichaEL Sawdy, *The Signs of Our Times* (Plymouth, MI: Biblical Signs Publishing, 2018), 43-46.

CHAPTER NINE: THIRD TEMPLE AND TWO WITNESSES

1. Tim LaHaye, *Revelation Unveiled* (Grand Rapids, MI: Zondervan, 1999) 185-187.

CHAPTER TEN: 7TH TRUMPET – 7 VIALS – 7 PLAGUES

1. MichaEL Sawdy, *Even More Signs of Our Times* (Plymouth, MI: Biblical Signs Publishing, 2019), 65-66.

CHAPTER ELEVEN: BABYLON THE GREAT IS FALLEN

1. Dave Hunt, *A Woman Rides the Beast* (Eugene, OR: Harvest House Publishers, 1994).
2. MichaEL Sawdy, *The Signs of Our Times* (Plymouth, MI: Biblical Signs Publishing, 2018), 43-46.

CHAPTER TWELVE: ARMAGEDDON AND CHRIST'S RETURN

1. Chuck Missler, "Revelation Session 22 Ch 19 The Return Of The King," 2013, accessed September 2019, https://youtu.be/rXovydznzQg

EPILOGUE: A NEW HEAVEN AND A NEW EARTH

1. Hal Lindsey, *There's A New World Coming* (Ventura, CA: Vision House Publishers, 1973/Bantam Edition, 1975), 262.

Recommended Books for Further Study

Hunt, Dave, *A Woman Rides the Beast* (Eugene, OR: Harvest House Publishers, 1994).

LaHaye, Tim, *Revelation Unveiled* (Grand Rapids, MI: Zondervan, 1999).

Lindsey, Hal, *There's A New World Coming* (Ventura, CA: Vision House Publishers, 1973/Bantam Edition, 1975).

MacArthur, John, *Because the Time is Near* (Chicago, IL: Moody Publishers, 2007).

McGee, J. Vernon, *Revelation Chapters 6-13* (Nashville, TN: Thomas Nelson Publishers, 1991).

McGee, J. Vernon, *Revelation Chapters 14-22* (Nashville, TN: Thomas Nelson Publishers, 1991).

Missler, Dr. Chuck, *Prophecy 20/20* (Nashville, TN: Thomas Nelson Publishers, 2006).

Reagan, Dr. David, *God's Plan for the Ages* (McKinney, TX: Lamb & Lion Ministries, 2005).

Van Impe, Dr. Jack, *Revelation Revealed* (Troy, MI: Jack Van Impe Ministries, 1982).

From the Author

I, MichaEL Sawdy, in no way intended to "add unto" or "take away from" the words of *The Revelation to St. John the Divine* in the writing of this book.

I penned this book as a commentary on what has long been one of the most difficult books of the Holy Bible for Christians to understand. It is meant to be used as a study tool that is read alongside the Bible, and is by no means meant to serve as a substitute or replacement for the Word of God. I urge everyone who has read this book to read and study the entire *Book of Revelation* for yourself - every chapter, verse, and word. For there are blessings promised to all who take the time to do so (Revelation 1:3).

ABOUT THE AUTHOR

MICHAEL SAWDY is the Author of the *Signs of Our Times* book series, and is also Founder of the *Biblical Signs In The Headlines* website. He had a life-changing experience with Jesus Christ in 2006, which led him to turn from a sinful life and fully dedicate his life to the Lord. Since then, he has spent thousands of hours studying the Bible; along with Biblical teachings by some of his greatest influences: the Benham Brothers (Jason and David), Jack Van Impe, Chuck Missler, Billy Graham, and John Hagee.

Due to the message which he'd received from the Lord during his salvation experience, MichaEL believes strongly that the Lord Jesus Christ is truly coming back down soon. This belief inspired him to create *BiblicalSigns.com* in 2015, and to write these books on Biblical Prophecy - specifically concerning the Rapture of the Church. His website surpassed over one-million visitors in 2017, and his books have all been #1 Best Sellers in multiple Christian Book categories on Amazon.

VISIT THE WEBSITE:
BiblicalSigns.com
FOLLOW ON SOCIAL MEDIA:
Facebook - /BiblicalSignsInTheHeadlines
/TheSignsOfOurTimesBook
Twitter - @MichaelofYHWH (Personal)
@BiblicalSigns (Website)
@SignsOfTimes777 (Books)

Get MichaEL's Best-Selling books -

THE SIGNS OF OUR TIMES: 12 Biblical Reasons Why This Could Be the Generation of the Rapture

EVEN MORE SIGNS OF OUR TIMES: More Biblical Reasons Why This Could Be the Generation of the Rapture

on Amazon, Audible, Barnes & Noble, Books-A-Million, iTunes, Walmart, or many other online book retailers around the world.

Made in the USA
Middletown, DE
20 December 2020

29210523R00086